Mike

and the inspiration
that is everywhere

Sidd

BRUNO MUNARI   THE CIRCLE

THE CIRCLE

While the square is closely linked to man and his constructions, to architecture, harmonious structures, writing, and so on, the circle is related to the divine: a simple circle has since ancient times represented eternity, since it has no beginning and no end. An ancient text says that God is a circle whose centre is everywhere but whose circumference is nowhere.
The circle is essentially unstable and dynamic: all rotary movements and impossible searches for perpetual motion derive from the circle.
Despite being the simplest of the curves, it is considered by mathematicians as a polygon with an infinite number of sides. If you remove an invisible point from the circumference of a circle then it is no longer a circle but a patho-circle, which presents complicated problems. A point marked on its circumference eliminates the idea of eternity, indicating a beginning and therefore an end to the circumference itself. If this circle rotates on the flat, the point marked

on its circumference describes a cycloid. The circle is easy to find in nature, all you have to do is throw a stone into still water. Instead, the sphere appears spontaneously in soap bubbles. Trees grow following a concentric circular pattern: a section shows its rings.

A circle drawn by hand showed the skill of Giotto. The first thing a child draws looks like a circle. People spontaneously arrange themselves in a circle when they need to observe something close up, and this led to the origin of the arena, the circus and the stock exchange trading posts.

One of the oldest symbols is a disk made up of two dynamic equal and opposing parts: Yang-Yin, which represent the balance of opposing forces in all living things.

Famous painters have painted on a circular surface, each of them finding compositional solutions closely tied to the circular shape. In certain cases, such as in Botticelli's Virgin with Child, the final effect of the work appears spherical to the eye.

A disk lying on a flat surface cannot be placed wrongly, which is why plates are almost always round; and it is easier to arrange them on the table. If they were hexagonal or square or oval it would require greater care to lay them out without creating a sense of disorder. A circle instead is always tidy. This is even truer of the sphere, which cannot be overturned in any way. A sphere is always the right way up, so to speak, in any position.

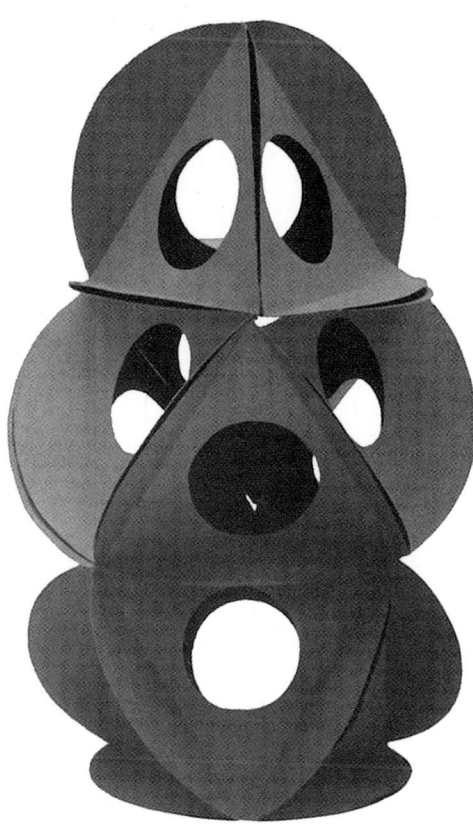

AGRIPPA

The magic circle of Agrippa.

AMATERAS

Popular Japanese divinity dressed in red and standing on a rock with the solar disk of the sun in her right hand. According to legend Amatéras was born from the left eye of the god Izanagui; from the moment she was born her resplendent beauty lit up the whole world and Izanagui gave her the empire of the sun.

ACONA' BICONBI'

Three dimensional construction obtained by repeating and joining equal elements in the shape of a circular crown. The overall shape changes depending on the number of elements used.

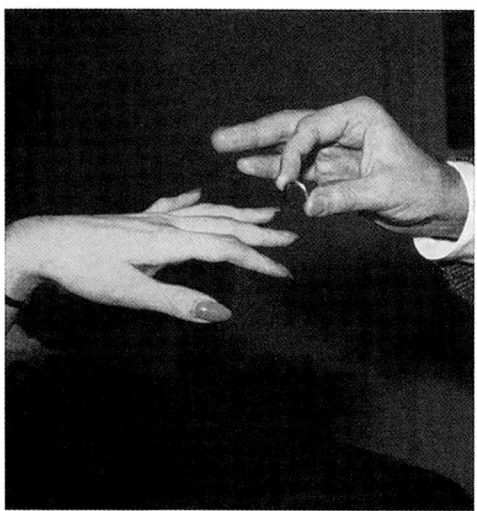

THE ARCHANGEL MICHAEL

The magic circle of the Archangel Michael.

THE RING

The ring is said to originate from Asia. Both Hebrews and Egyptians wore rings. Initially the Romans only wore iron rings with a seal. Gold rings were the mark of people of high birth.
Each year, during the reign of Pope Alexander III, the Venetian Doges would throw a ring into the sea on Ascension Day to symbolise a marriage with the sea.

GROWTH RINGS

A cross-section of a tree trunk.

HALO

Portrait of St Francis by Simone Martini, Assisi.

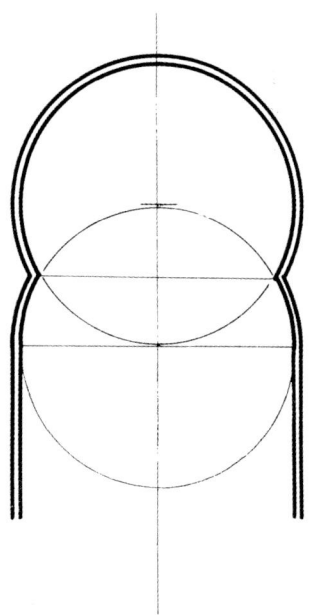

MUSLIM ARCH

Structural outline of an Arabian-Moorish arch.

NEWTON'S RINGS

If you put a slightly convex lens lit by a white light on a flat piece of glass a series of concentric iridescent rings appear at the spot where the two pieces of glass meet. If you use a red light instead of a white one a large number of concentrated, regular rings, alternately red and dark, form around the point of contact; as you gradually move away from the black spot in the centre, the distance between the rings diminishes. Newton discovered that the radii of the dark rings are the same as the square roots of consecutive even numbers.

TO HAVE FINISHED

After a sacrifice the ancients would make a circle in the altar using the blood of the victims collected in a jar and then they would pronounce a holy Greek word meaning to *have finished*.

ANNUAL - BIENNIAL

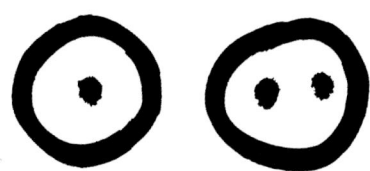

Botanical signs for annual or biennial plants.

EQUAL AREAS

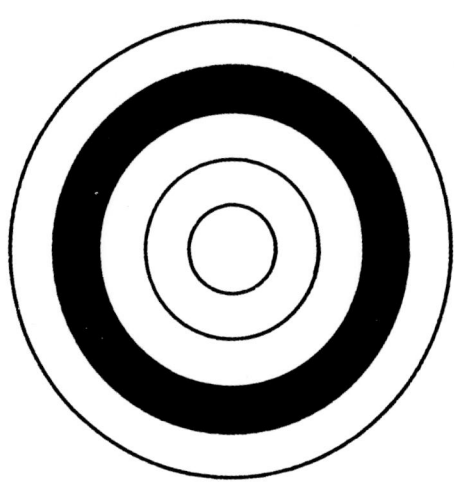

The surface outside the black ring, contained within a wider circumference, is equal to the surface inside the black ring. The radius is divided into five equal parts.

JAPANESE FLAG

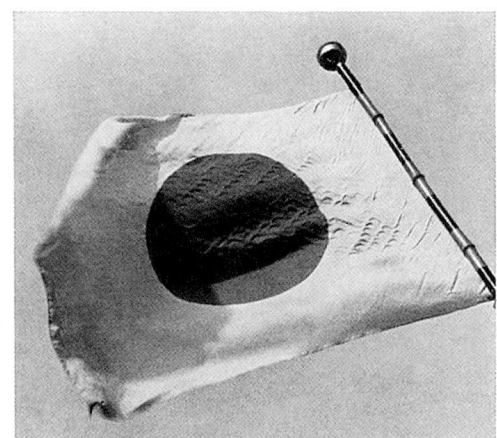

OLYMPIC FLAG

DAVIDE BORIANI

Magnetic surface. Kinetic object, shown at the Exhibition of Programmed Art, Olivetti, May 1962, Milan. The object measures 80 cm in diameter and contains iron powder kept in constant movement by a number of magnets that move in different ways underneath the surface, making an infinite number of patterns.

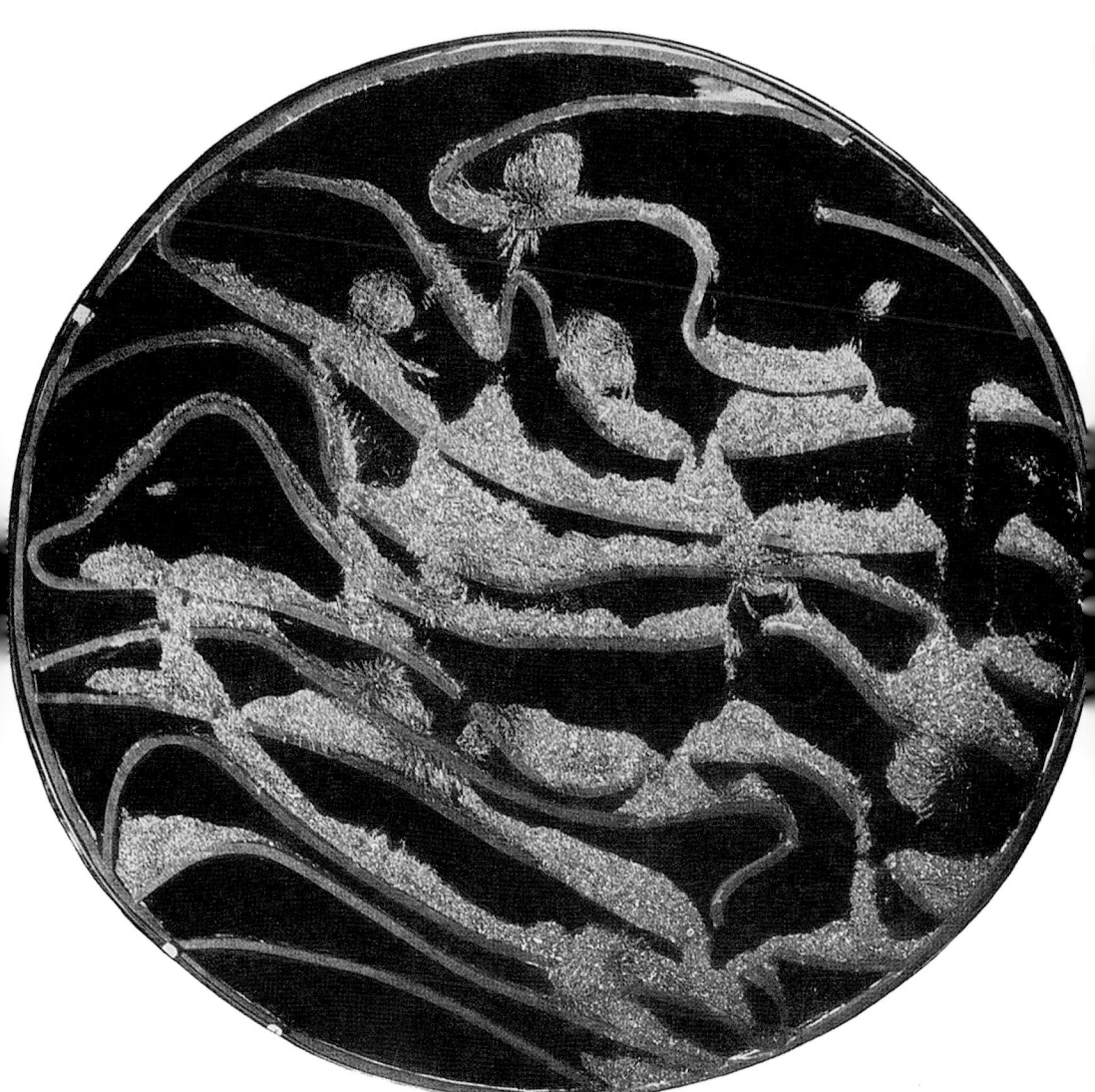

BAPTISTERY

The Baptistery at Pisa, one of the most beautiful old buildings on a circular base.

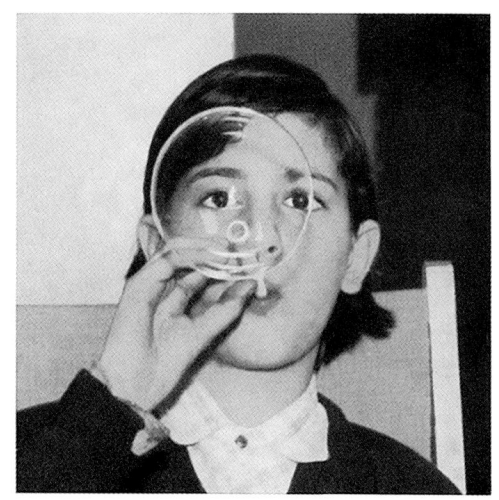

SOAP BUBBLES

A natural sphere.

MAX BILL

Design made from a series of circles. 1942.

THE STOCK EXCHANGE

A circular trading post at the Stock Exchange.

BOWLS

A game of bowls at Monte Olimpino.

GOOD SPIRITS

A magic circle to attract Good Spirits.

BOTTICELLI

The Virgin and Child. Uffizi Gallery, Florence. The particular composition and painting technique give the round surface of the painting the impression of being a sphere.

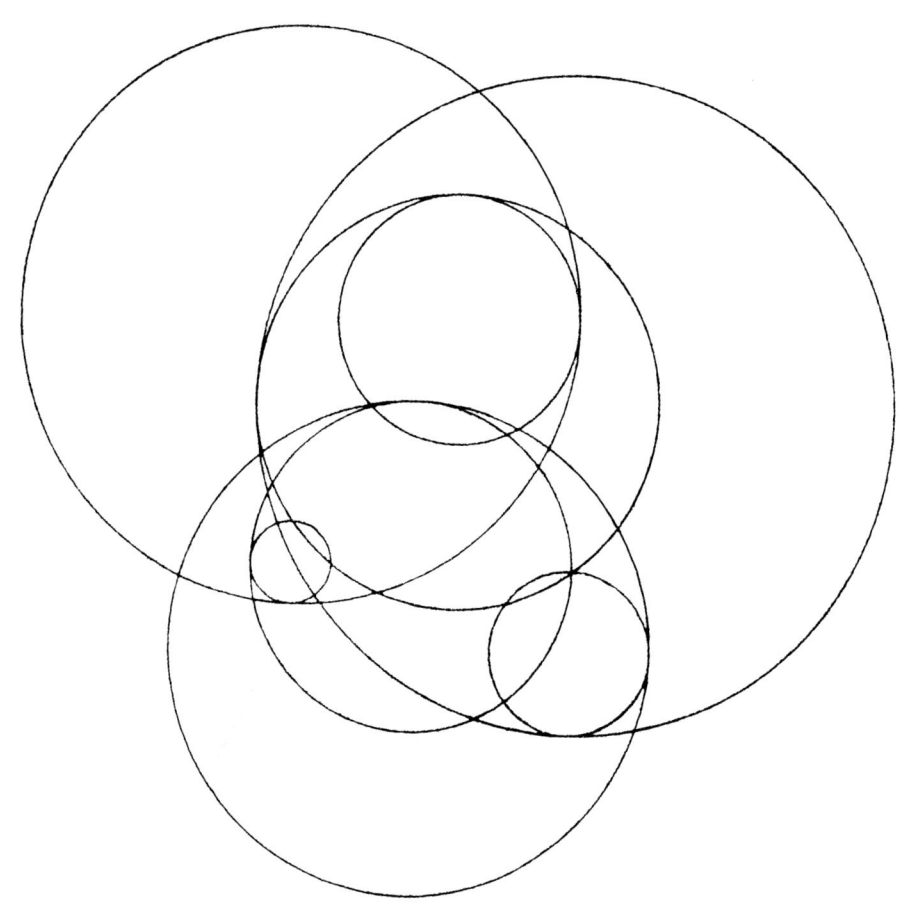

LANFRANCO BOMBELLI

Drawing, 1947.

ROUND HUT

The two oldest types of dwelling have either a square or a round ground plan. The domed hut is found in Australia and among many African and American peoples.

BALL BEARING

A MATAKAM HOUSE

At Mokolo in the Cameroon are the houses of the Matakam. Each room is cylindrical and made of beaten earth crowned by a conical thatched roof. The rooms form a large enclosure. Each room has a specific function; the number of rooms is determined by the number of family members. There are no openings for the light to enter the rooms and one circulates as if in a dark circular maze.

Enclosure for a family of nineteen members with the room (or house) of the head of the family; house for the bull, house for the main wife, houses for the other wives and children, house for the oldest married son, house for an adult son, house for the water tank, the kitchen, houses for the goats, larders, the tank for the ashes with which salt is made, the outer wall. The Matakam keep the bull walled up in its house and it can only communicate with the outside through a small, very low opening through which it cannot pass. There is another opening for scraping out the manure. The bull is kept like this for three years, during which time it is fed and looked after. It is let out on the feast of the ancestors and killed in a solemn ceremony performed under the direction of the Bull Master.

CARDIOID

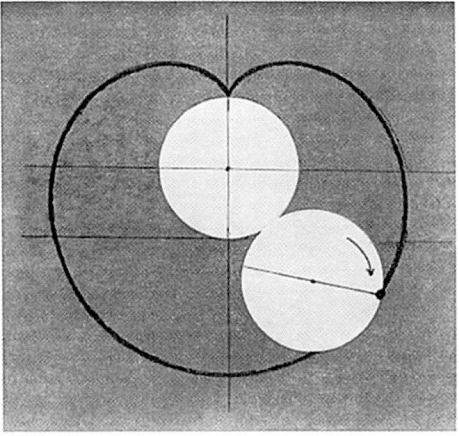

A curve described by a point situated on a circle which rolls, without slipping, around the circumference of another circle.

CYCLOID

The cycloid is the path traced by a fixed point on the circumference of a circle that rolls along a given straight line. An interesting property of the cycloid was discovered by Galileo: with the help of the cycloid we can construct an area that is exactly the same as that of the given circle. First of all the length of the cycloid from cusp to cusp is equal to four times the length of the diameter of the generating circle. On the basis of this it can be demonstrated that the area delimited by the portion of the cycloid between the two cusps and the straight line that unites them is equal to three times the area of the circle. Therefore the space delimited by each part of the circle is exactly the same as the area of the circle itself.

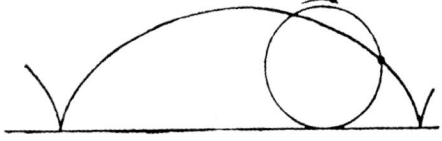

Astrological circles to calculate configurations.

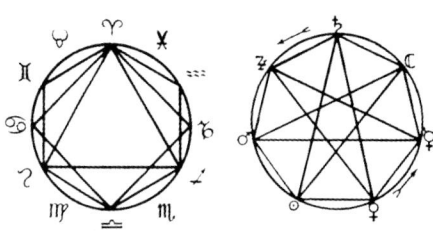

COMPASSES

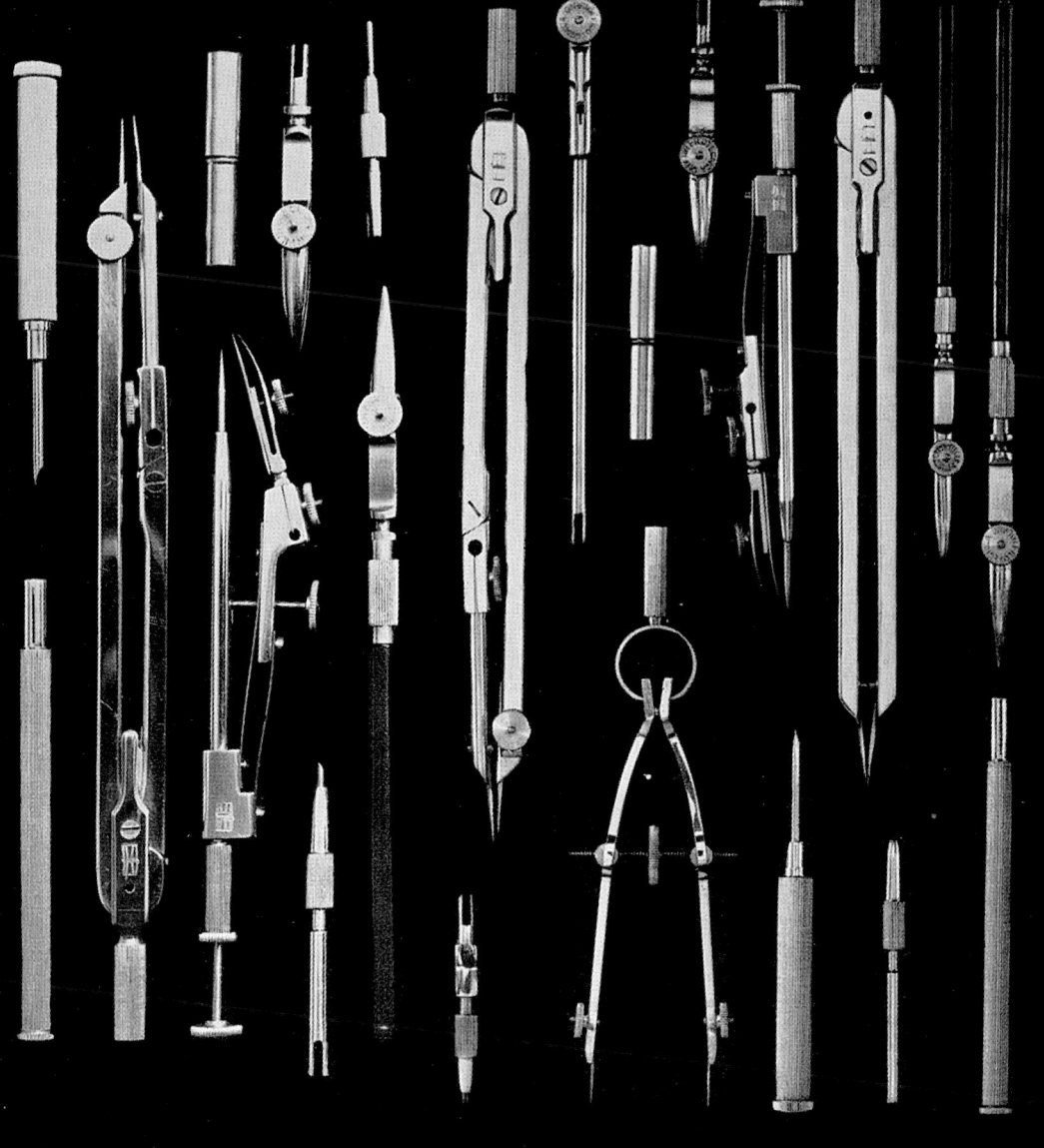

CURTATE CYCLOID

A point traced out on the inside of a circle rolling along a straight line generates a curtate cycloid.

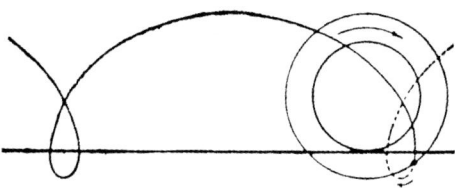

PROLATE CYCLOID

A point on the outside of a circle rolling along a straight line describes a prolate cycloid.

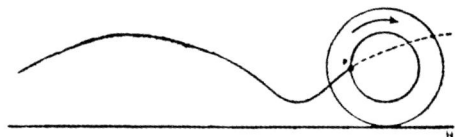

CLEOPATRA

Cleopatra's magic circle.

CYCLE

A concept introduced by Laguerre: the cycle is a circle with an arrow marked on its circumference. An equal circle with the arrow facing in the opposite direction is another, different cycle.

CLUSTERS OF SPHERES

The thickest cluster of spheres is obtained when the centres of the spheres form a rhombohedric network.

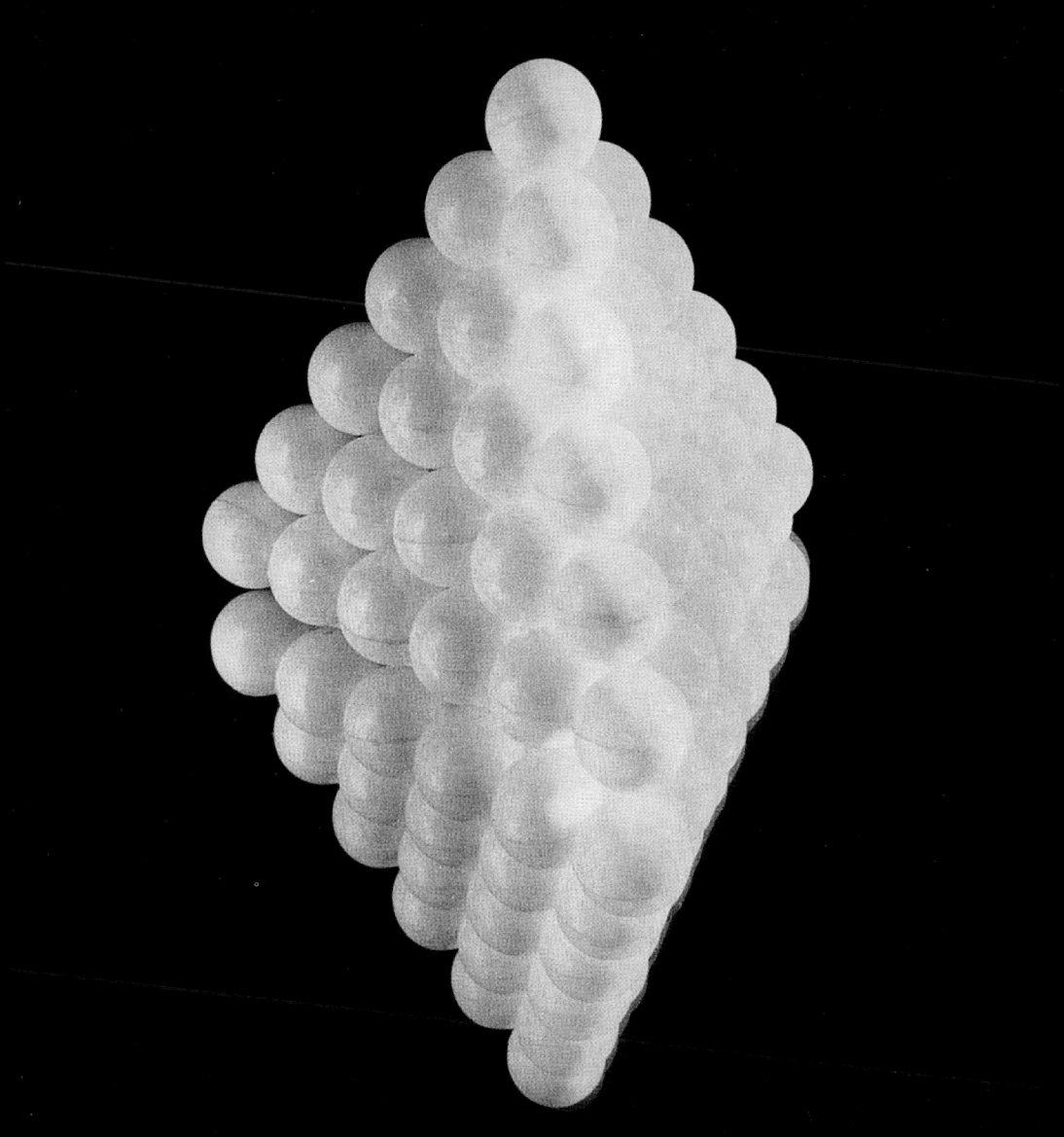

THE POLYGONAL CIRCLE

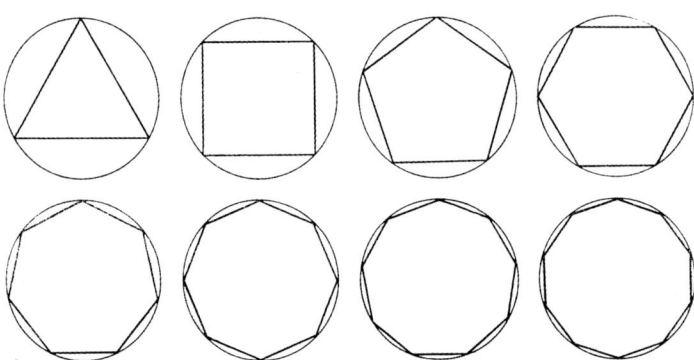

Circles with inscribed polygons. The same is true for circumscribed polygons. The method of increasing or decreasing polygons was known to Archimedes who, using 96-sided polygons, demonstrated that π is less than 3 1/7 and more than 3 10/71. The area of the circle is to be found between these two figures.

OPPOSITION

Two circles that touch, like two wheels that move in the opposite direction when they make contact, symbolise opposition.

THE MAGIC CIRCLE OF THE COVENANT

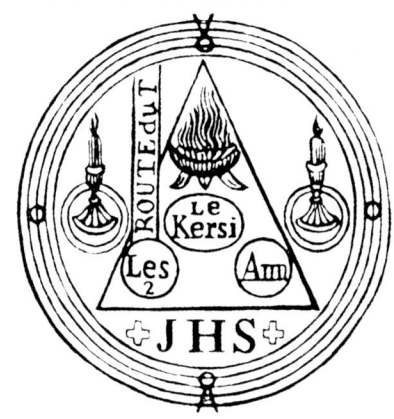

CONE SPHERE

Model of experimental geometry made by the School of Ulm.

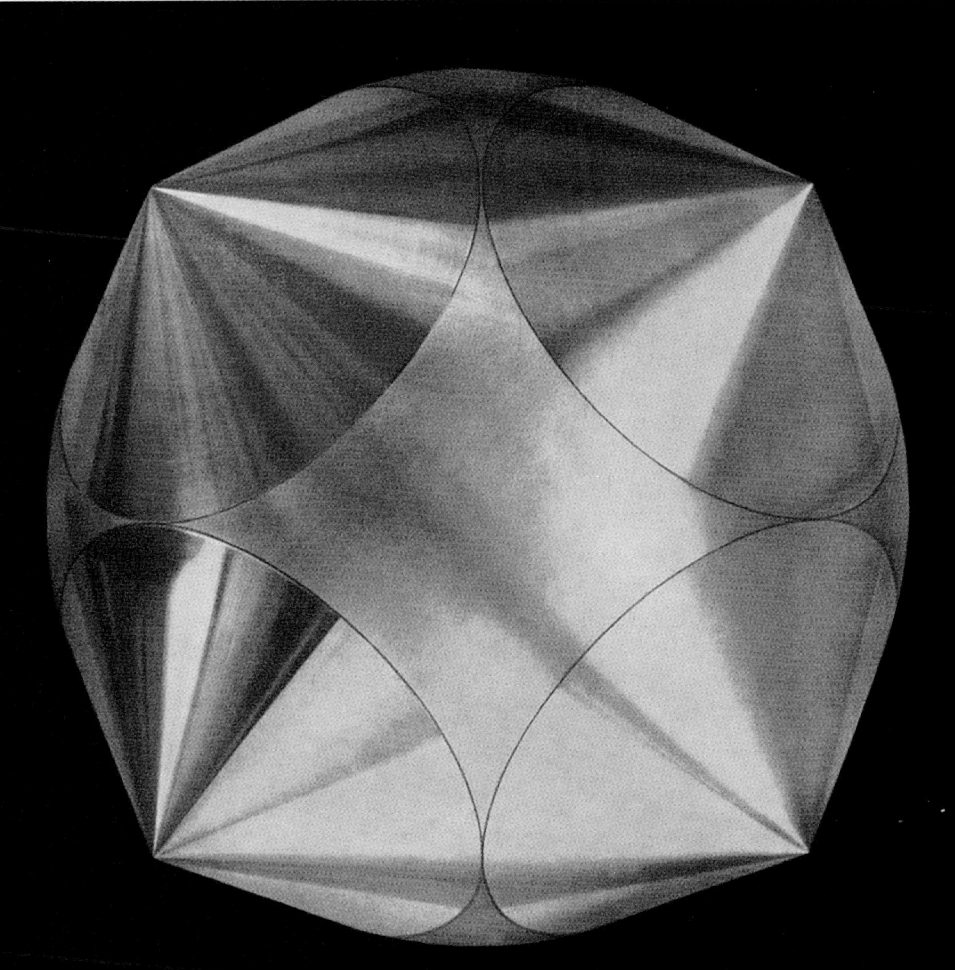

HORSE POWER

A wheel in which a horse produces power by walking along its internal circumference. This was used in the past to move the paddles on the river boats. In China dogs were used to move the wheels of small mills and prisoners were used to bring water up to irrigate the fields.

CIRCLE

The circle is one of the oldest figures in mathematics. The straight line is the simplest of lines but the circle is the simplest curve.

CURVES INSIDE AND OUT

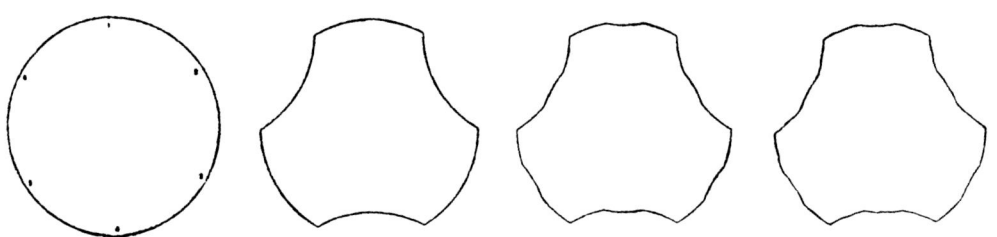

Draw a circle with any radius and choose six equidistant points on the circumference. Take three alternate arcs and turn them inwards. The perimeter remains the same. Then trisect each internal or external arc and invert the central section. By continuing this operation we obtain a final curve whose perimeter is equal to the original circle and an area equal to the inscribed hexagon.

INSCRIBED CIRCLES

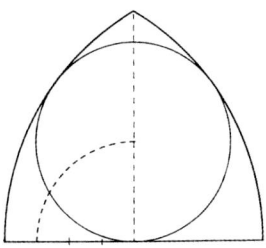

Inscribe a circle in a mixtilinear isosceles triangle.

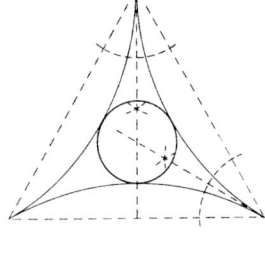

Inscribe a circle in a curvilinear equilateral triangle with concave sides.

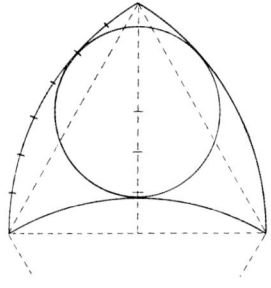

Inscribe a circle in a curvilinear equilateral triangle of which three sides are convex and one is concave.

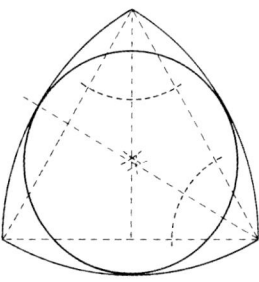

Inscribe a circle in a curvilinear equilateral triangle with convex sides.

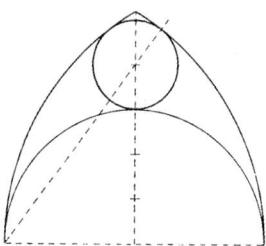

Inscribe a circle in a curvilinear triangle having as sides a semicircle and two arcs whose radii are equal to the diameter of the semicircle itself.

DECORATION

DIFFRACTION

Diffraction of electrons through a very thin layer of silver. This is proves the wave nature of the electron, and therefore of matter.

DANCE

Dancing in a circle, beating rhythmically, no one is first, no one last, all are the same, all beat in the same way. The start is slow then the rhythm takes over, a sense of infinity arises from this human ring that turns and beats rhythmically. Photo Michel Huet.

VILLARD DE HONNECOURT

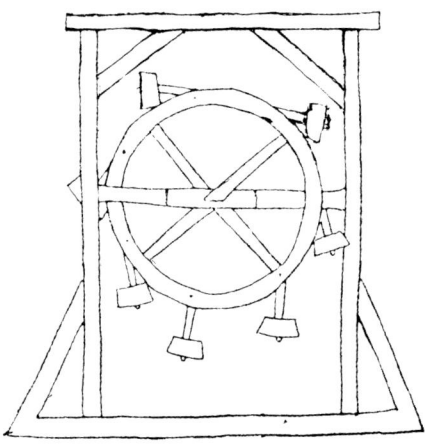

One of the first drawings of a perpetual motion machine.

THE SUN GOD

The religion of ancient Egypt was based on the adoration of the sun. The form of the Sun God Amon-Râ was a hawk or a man with the appearance of a hawk with a solar disk, travelling through the sky. An ancient chant of Thebes says: Amon-Râ, divine hawk with shining plumage, traces with the spread of his wings a circle on the vault of the skies.
Amenophis IV, according to hieroglyphic interpretation, started a new cult with the adoration of the real sun in place of the God Ammon-Râ. Since then the sun god is simply represented by a radiant disk.

GOD

"God is a circle whose centre is everywhere but whose circumference is nowhere". Old saying.

MAXWELL'S DISK

A turquoise and red disk in different adjustable parts. By rotating this disk you obtain a neutral grey colour. The neutral shade of grey depends on the two colours being exactly complementary. If the amount of red is greater, you get a reddish grey and if the turquoise is greater the result will be a bluish green.

CHROMATIC DISK

Diagram of complementary colours on a chromatic disk. The numbers marked by a small square indicate the relative positions of the colours on the normal spectrum and the numbers marked by a cross indicate the wavelengths in ten-millionths of a millimetre.

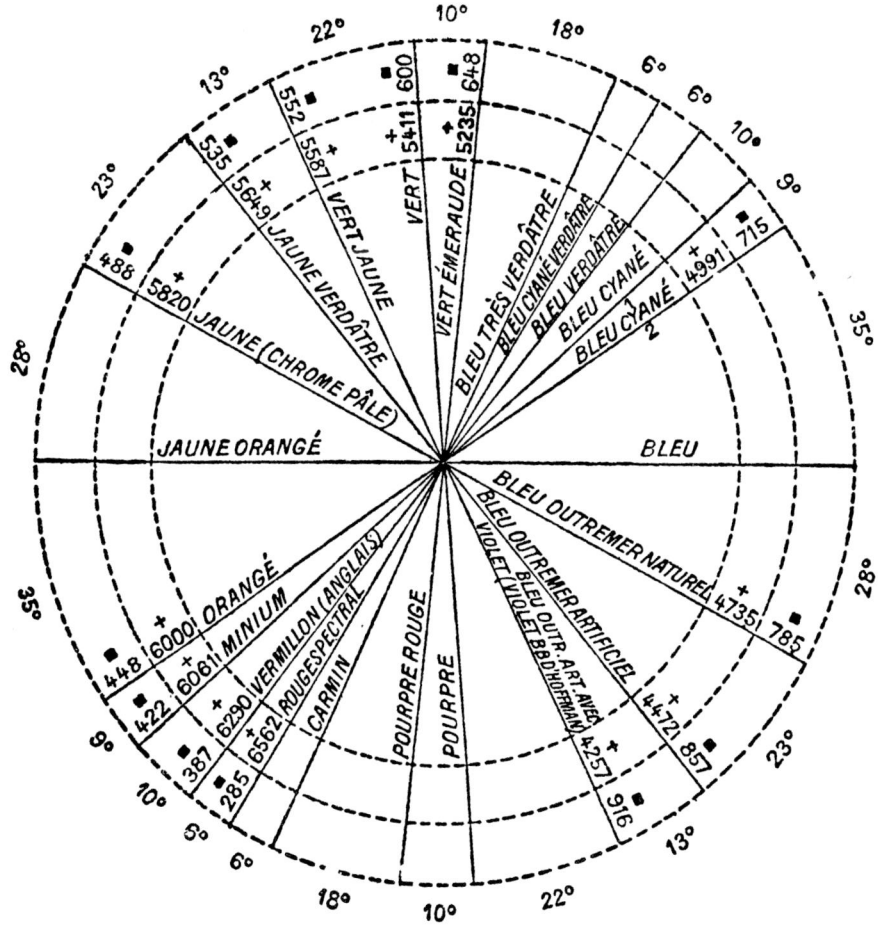

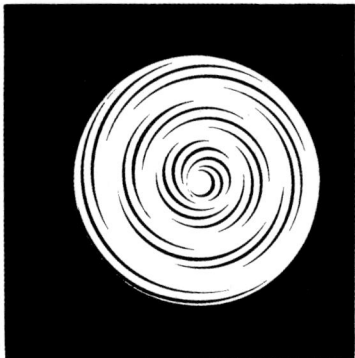

MARCEL DUCHAMP

Disks rotating at a constant speed with special optical effects, devised by Marcel Duchamp in 1936.

MUSLIM DECORATION

Muslim decoration at Constantinople.

NEWTON'S DISK

A wheel made up of sections of different sizes in all the colours of the spectrum, repeated four times. By rotating the disk at speed all the colours blend into a luminous white.

COMPOSITIONS

Some examples of figures obtained with circles, disks and parts of them.

ETERNITY

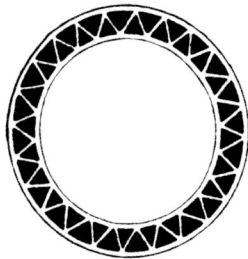

Eastern eternity symbol.

The snake biting its tail is a symbol of eternity.

BENHAM'S DISK

Take a white disk and cover half of it in deep black, then paint concentric bands on the other half. When it rotates at a certain speed you will notice how instead of seeing concentric grey rings, there are coloured bands, dark and of low saturation. This leads us to the disconcerting conclusion made by S. I. Vavilov that we cannot base ourselves simply on visual perception to define light.

ACUSTIC EXPERIMENTS

In the US experiments have been made on the sound effects inside a sphere large enough to contain a person. The sound transmitted by the walls makes the whole body resonate: skull, thorax, abdominal cavity and bones all vibrate at once. To the man, it seems that the sound derives from his body. The musical experience is activated to the full, although the man remains passive. His body resounds and a readiness to assimilate and individual will are of little importance.

OPTICAL EFFECT

BUCKMINSTER FULLER

One of the many geodesic domes designed by Fuller. In 1957 it took 22 hours to build this enormous dome in Honolulu for a series of concerts. All geodesic domes are built using prefabricated parts and are easily assembled. In certain cases, some domes were hung from a metal cable and transported by helicopter. Fuller created geodesic domes in a wide range of different materials, plastic, wood and at the Milan Triennal of 1954 he made one out of cardboard with a radius of approximately ten metres.

SPHERICAL BUILDINGS

In around 1770 Claude-Nicolas Ledoux designed a giant sphere as a symbol of eternity for the cemetery of Caux. He also designed a spherical home for the caretakers as a symbol of human solitude. In 1800 Lequeu designed a spherical "Temple of the Earth". Later, the Russian composer and theosophist Aleksandr Skrjabin designed a semi-spherical building which would stand over the water so that its reflection would complete the other half of the sphere. The building was to be constructed in India and was to be the site of a holy play about universal redemption. Russian architects, who tended towards futurism, designed a suspended spherical building to be used as a planetarium and reading room for the Lenin Institute. In March 1958 Johann Ludovici submitted a spherical house made of metal to the London Exhibition.

BALANCE

The three stages of balance of a wheel: with the weight at the top it is unstable. With the weight at the bottom it is stable. With the weight in the centre, it is neutral. Spontaneous motion can only arise in the first case. This principle is always put into practice for models of machines for perpetual motion.

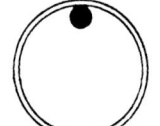

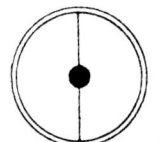

CYLINDRICAL FOUNTAIN

The outer cylinder is 2 metres high with a diameter of 4 metres. It is made of iron with panels of coloured plastic material curved like the blades

of a turbine. The other two inner cylinders are built on the same principle. The outer cylinder is activated by a slow motor and its colours are neutral, from black to white. The medium cylinder turns with the wind and its colours are warm and transparent, from yellow to purple and red. The small cylinder is propelled by a jet of water and its colours are cold, from green to blue. The random blending of these colours as the cylinders rotate creates unexpected effects.
Built for Montecatini at the Milan Fair 1961.

SPHERICAL GEOMETRY

When establishing his non-Euclidian principles of geometry, Lobacevskij began with the definition of the distance between two points as an invariant of movement; then on the basis of the definition of the distance between two points he was able to add the definition of the surface of the sphere as a locus of the points in space equidistant from a given point. The definition of the circle or, to be exact, the circumference, follows on from that of the spherical surface in that the circle is defined as a locus of the points common to two spherical surfaces. It follows then that the plane can be defined as a locus of the circles of intersection of spheres having the same radius described around two fixed points which are also poles of the plane. In this way Lobacevskij defined a limited portion of the plane, the one inside the generating circle. The infinity of the plane exists not as a fact but as the possibility of extending the area in all directions. Lastly, he defined the straight line as the intersection of two planes; or rather the segment of a straight line as the diameter common to two great circles of a sphere.

YELLOW AND DEEP BLUE

In his book "Concerning the Spiritual in Art" Kandinsky describes the optical effect of colours. He says that if you fill two circles of equal size, one yellow and one dark blue, you observe, after concentrating briefly on one and then the other, that the yellow radiates outwards and almost visibly comes closer to us. The blue on the other hand develops centripetally and moves away from us. The eye is struck by the yellow circle while it is drawn into the blue one.

TOYS AND GAMES

Many toys and games are based on the circle: ring-a-ring-a-roses, the merry-go-round, roulette, the hoop, the top, the ball, the pin-wheel and others.

PEOPLE IN A CIRCLE

People automatically arrange themselves in a circle when they want to look at something together. This probably gave rise to the form of the arena, the circus and the trading posts at the stock exchange. Photo by Lori Sammartino.

HINDU

Cosmic Hindu diagram.

IGLOO

The home of the Eskimo is a hollow half-sphere made with blocks of snow. A long open corridor leading outside provides ventilation while protecting the entrance from cold winds.
It is said that 'a new hut is warmer than an old one because it is made of snow, while an old hut is made of ice'. Although it takes longer to build an igloo than a tropical hut, it is only a temporary home for hunters and is abandoned in spring when the snow on the roof starts to melt and when the puddles on the floor make it inhabitable. Photo by Mario De Biasi.

JOSEPH

Joseph's problem is certainly one of the most famous and one of the oldest. Depending on the era in which the story is set, the people are either Christians and Jews, Christians and Turks, blacks and whites, good and bad. The original story was about Joseph, who found himself in a cave with 40 other Jews firmly decided on killing themselves rather than face an even worse fate at the hands of the Romans. Joseph, who had decided to save his own skin, arranged them in a circle and established to general agreement that counting in threes around the circle, the person who was third, sixth etc would be killed. In the circle of 41 people he kept 16th and 31st place for himself and for another farsighted person. Although he and his companion remained to the end they were able to avoid martyrdom.

Another version of this problem has 15 Turks and 15 Christians on board a ship tossed by a storm; the ship would sink unless half the passengers were thrown into the sea. After arranging everyone in a circle, the Christians suggested that the every ninth, eighteenth etc person would be killed. Naturally enough, the infidels were arranged so as to spare all the Christians.

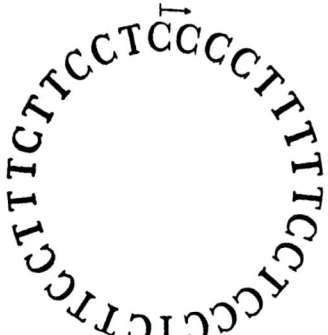

LEONARDO DA VINCI

Variations on Leonardo's principle of the perpetual motion machine based on free-moving spheres.

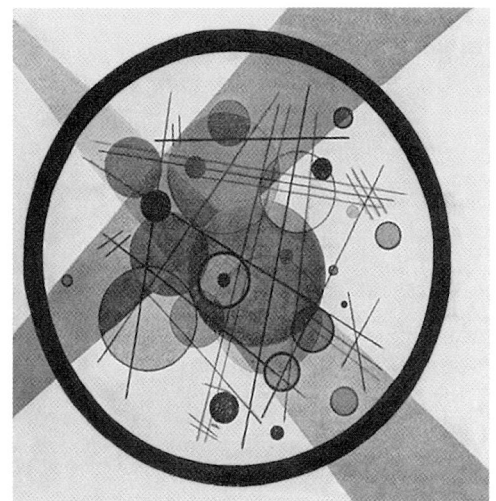

KANDINSKY

Circles within a circle, painting 1923. Louise and Walter Arensberg Collection. Philadelphia Museum of Art.

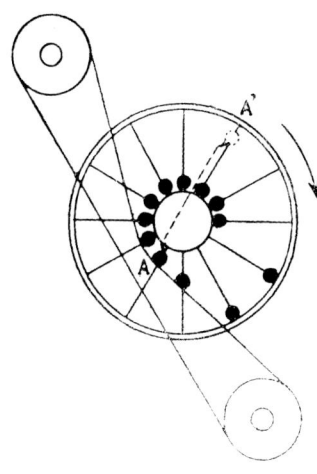

PAUL KLEE

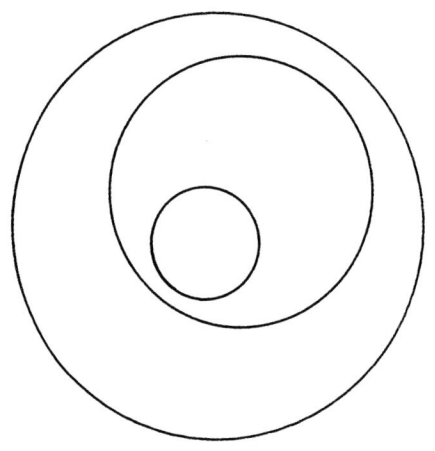

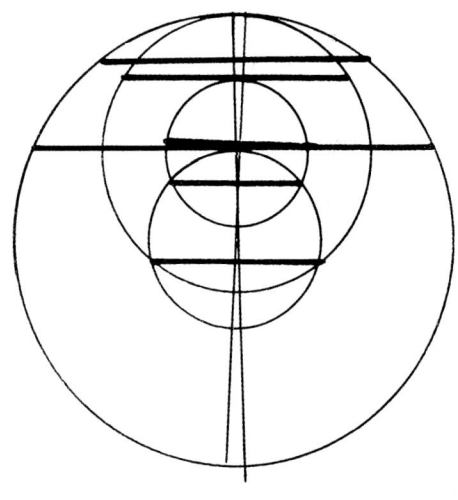

Movement and counter-movement.

Sensitisation of layers as the centre changes position. The raising of the point of vision always involves the raising of the horizon line.

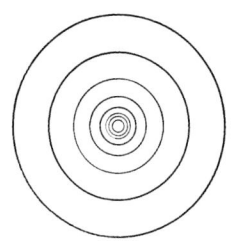
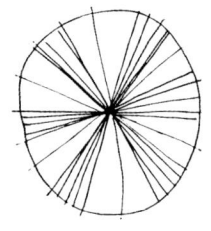

Patterns of energy formation of the circle by radiation from the centre and by the progressive growth of the radius from the inside to the outside.

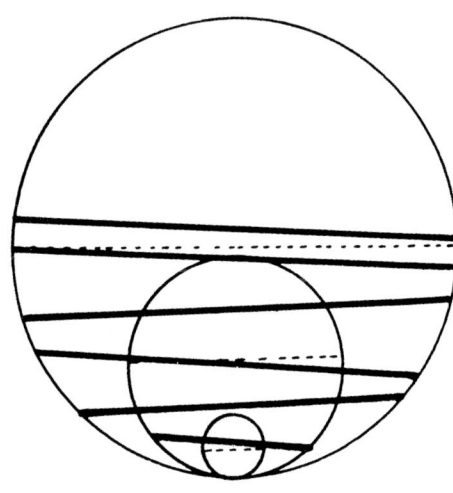

Synthesis of static and dynamic relationships.

FRANÇOIS MORELLET

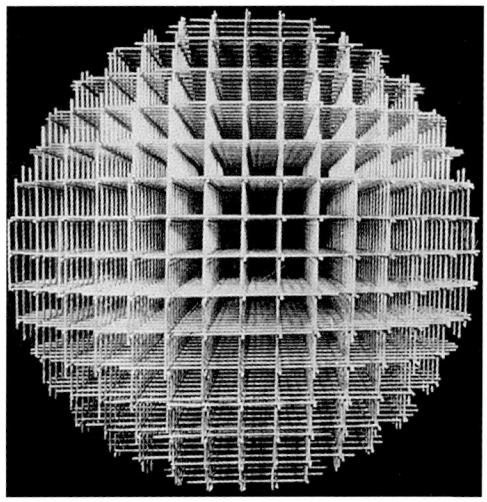

Spherical object obtained by soldering a series of metal rods of different sizes at right angles. Depending on the point of observation the object either appears as a sphere with a cubic structure or a hexagonal one.

MANDALA

A symbol of totality. There are many versions of it: from the so-called prehistoric "circle of the sun", to the circle that surrounds and protects, to the alchemist's microcosm and, lastly, as the modern symbol that contains psychic entirety.

RING MACHINE

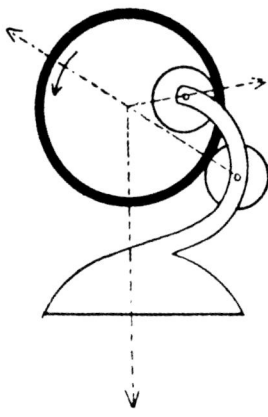

An iron ring is held by two cylinders attached to a curved arm. The ring is free and according to the inventor it should turn and therefore make the cylinders turn, because the force of gravity will draw it downwards. However the centre of gravity of the ring always stays in the same place so that the machine acquires perfect, immobile equilibrium.

MICHELANGELO

The Holy Family. Uffizi Gallery, Florence.

BYZANTINE MONOGRAM

MERCURY MACHINE

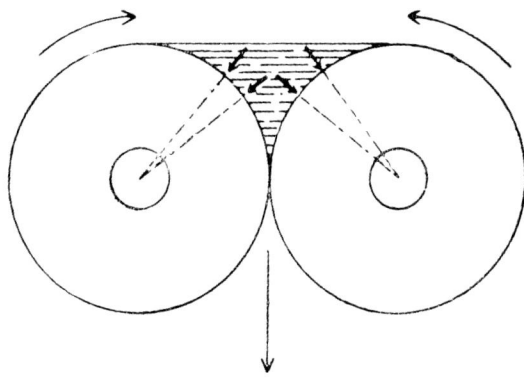

Two cylinders in perfect contact with each other and rotating in opposite directions inside a sealed box. The mercury has been placed in the upper, shaded part and this should put pressure on the cylinders, making them turn. All liquids put pressure on the bottom of the recipient in which they are contained but in this case the recipient has no bottom but only walls. Therefore the pressure is put on the walls and, because it is directed towards the centre of the cylinders, these remain still.

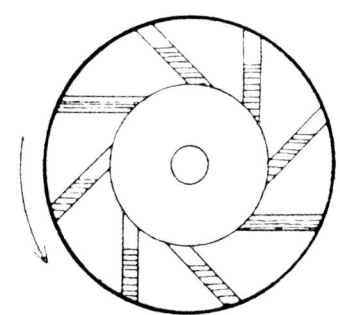

HYDROSTATIC MACHINE

Diagram for perpetual motion with liquid weight.

MACHINE WITH SPHERES

ENZO MARI

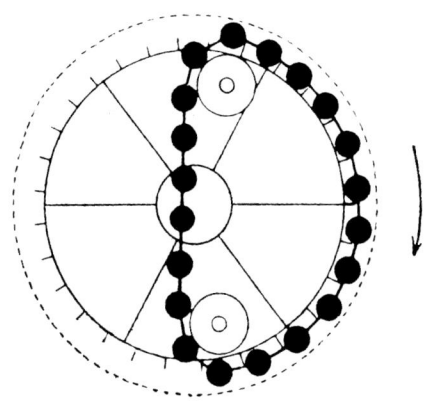

Perpetual motion machine.
Being greater than the weight of the other spheres, the weight of the sphere around the curve ought to bring about the motion.

Composition no. 383. Aluminium and laminated plastic, 67x23x20 cm, black, white and blue. 1959.

Phenolic resin sphere containing cubic meshing. Structure no. 969, diameter 12 cm.

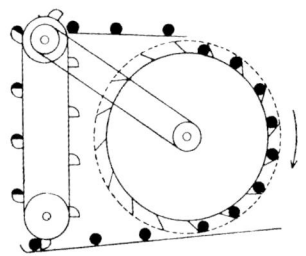

Variation of the same principle.

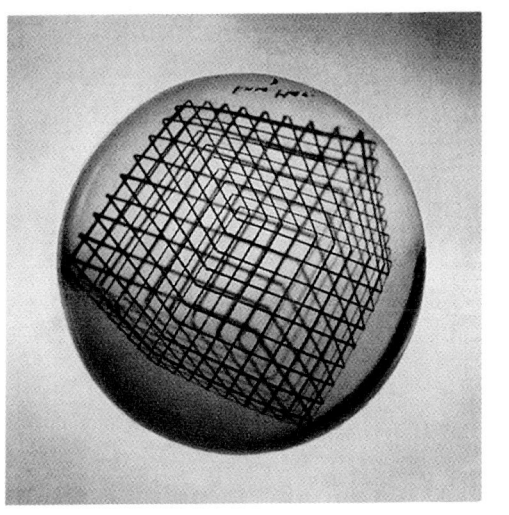
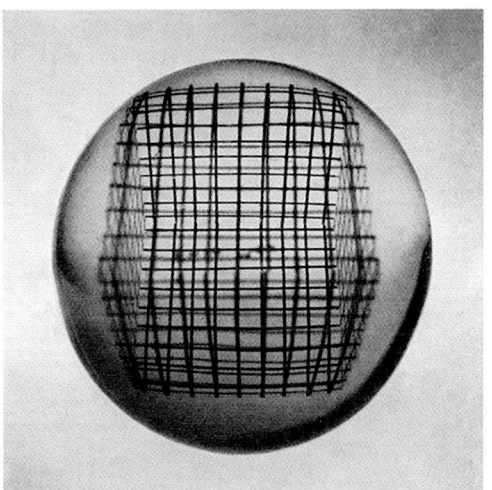
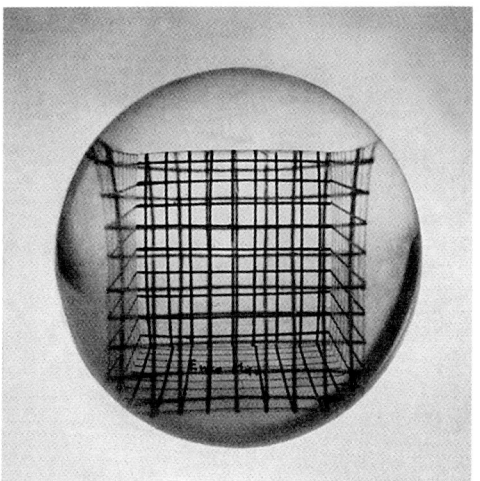
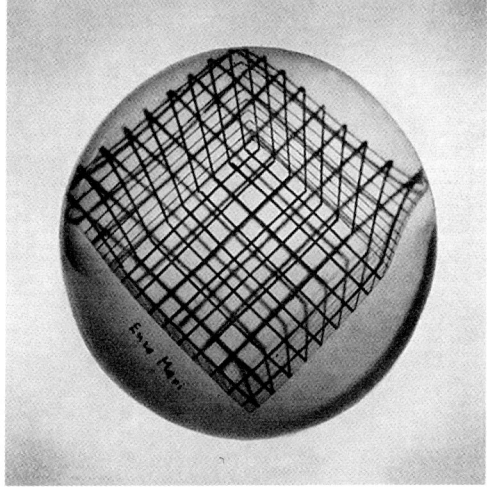

TRADEMARKS

Symbols and trademarks either round in shape or made up of elements deriving from the circle.

WATCH

The turning of the hands determines the most logical shape of this object.

NURAGHI

Ancient Sardinian constructions from the Bronze Age or perhaps earlier. They have a round base and are built with large stones. Some are as high as 16 metres tall with a base diameter of about 30 metres which then tapers towards the top.

EIGHT CIRCLES

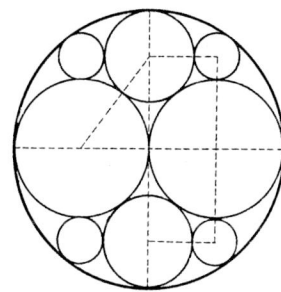

In a given circle inscribe eight circles of different sizes, placed symmetrically and tangent to each other and to the given circle.

GIOTTO'S O

At Pisa Giotto made such a marvellous painting that... "the work brought him in that city and elsewhere such fame that pope Benedict IX, having the desire to carry out some paintings in St. Peter's, sent one of his courtiers from Trevisi to Tuscany to see what kind of man this Giotto was and what his works were like. The courtier on his way to see Giotto learned that there were in Florence other excellent masters in painting and mosaic, and spoke in Siena to many masters. Then, after obtaining drawings from them he went to Florence. Going one morning into the studio of Giotto who was at work, he described to him what the Pope had in mind and how he wished to make use of his work, and finally he asked him for a few drawings to send to His Holiness. Giotto, who was most well-mannered, took some paper and using a paintbrush dipped in red, held his arm still at the side like a compass and, turning his hand, drew a circle so perfect in curve and profile that it was a marvel to behold. After this, grinning at the courtier, he said: — Here is your drawing —. Thinking he was being mocked he said: — Will I have any other drawing besides this? — This is more than enough; — replied Giotto — send it along with the others and you will see that it will be well received.

"The envoy, seeing that he would be given no more, left most dissatisfied, and fearing that he had been tricked. Nevertheless, he sent the Pope the other drawings and the names of those who had done them. He also sent Giotto's drawing, explaining how he had drawn his circle without moving his arm and without using a compass. This is how the Pope and his many expert courtiers learned that Giotto's excellence far surpassed that of the other painters of his time. Once the news became known it gave origin to the saying still in use today about dim-witted men: "You are rounder than Giotto's O". This is a fine proverb not only due to the event which gave rise to it, but all the more so because its meaning is ambiguous, since in the Tuscan language the word tondo does not only mean 'perfect circle' but also one who is none too sharp.

"The Pope invited him to Rome where, praising him greatly and recognising his high merit, he engaged him to paint five stories of the life of Christ in the tribune of St Peter's, and to execute the main painting in the sacristy; he executed these works with such great diligence that no better work ever came from his hands. To reward his merit and as a sign of gratitude the Pope paid him six hundred gold ducats and bestowed upon him many favours, so that his name became known throughout Italy".

DEMOSTRATIVE OBJECT SKF

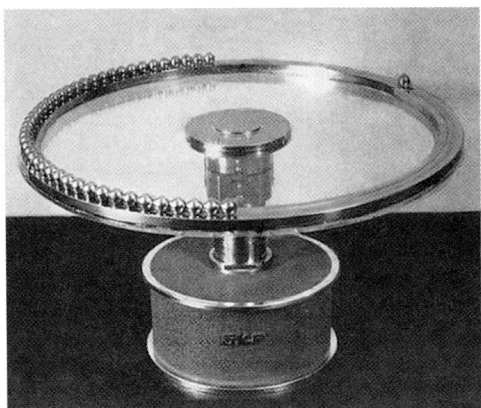

The large glass disk has a metal rim with a groove containing a number of steel balls. The disk is slightly inclined and it rotates very slowly so that every so often a ball separates from the top part and rolls half way round the circle until it joins up with the first ball at the other end. Immediately, another ball separates from the others and so on...

INITIAL POINT

If we put an initial point on the circumference of a circle we obtain a new figure which is used in the theory of polygene or complex functions.

GOLD

Magic circle used for making gold.

UMBRELLA

Japanese bamboo umbrella with waterproof varnished paper. The spokes of the umbrella come from a single bamboo cane. When the umbrella is closed the spokes fit back into the shape of the cane they were cut from and the umbrella is enclosed inside it.

GESTALT PSYCHOLOGY

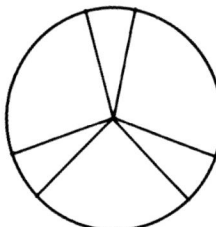

After staring for a while at the centre of this figure, most people suddenly see a different scheme. The radii that in the first drawing served as edges to the narrow sections become the edges of the wider sections. Clearly, the layout of the scheme has changed and it tends to change again. The rhythm at which the two figures alternate will gradually increase as the person stares at the centre of the figure.

ASTROLOGICAL PLANISPHERE

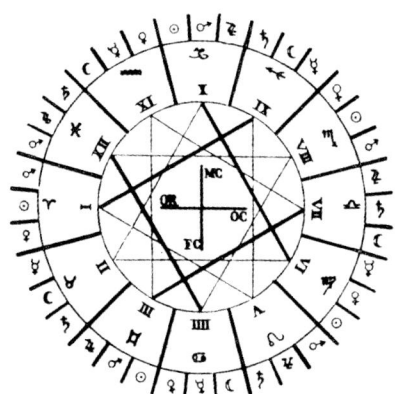

π

In the Book of Kings and in the Chronicles, π is given as 3. Egyptian mathematicians gave it the value of 3.16; the decimal 3.1416 was known at the time of Ptolemy in the year 150 BC.

PATHOCIRCLE

Another variation on the circle was introduced by the eminent American mathematician, C. J. Geyser. This consisted in taking a circle and removing a point from it. Although the figure cannot be drawn because a point has no extension, it was an important change in concept. Keyser called the new figure a pathocircle, meaning a pathological circle, and he used it to discuss the axioms of logic.

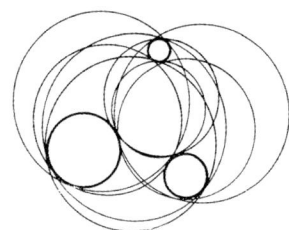

THE PROBLEM OF APOLLONIUS

Given three circles, find the circle tangent to them. The problem can be solved simply using ruler and compass and there are eight possible solutions.

CONCENTRIC WAVES

One of the natural forms of the circle.

POLAROID

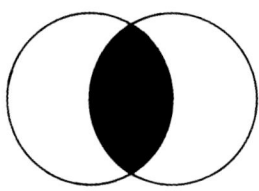

Graphic symbol of Polaroid filters.

PSEUDOSPHERE

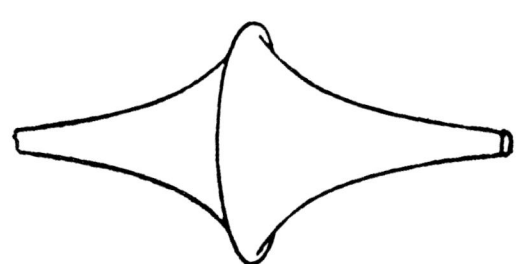

Geometric form determined by the rotation of a tractrix around the longitudinal axis. The tractrix is a curve perpendicular to a family of equal circles, placed at equal distances, whose centres are on a straight line.

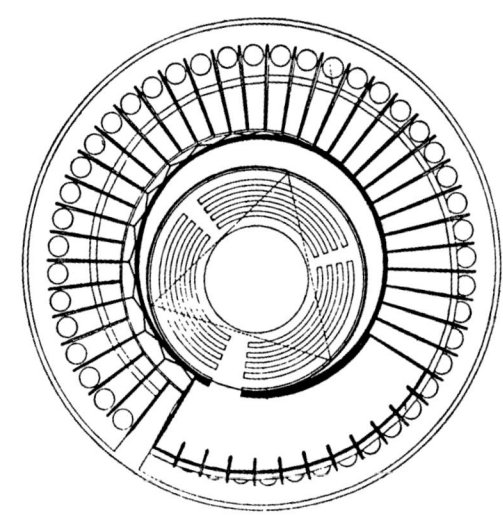

PAFFARD KEATINGE CLAY

Plan of a building to be used for experimental performances of dance, music and light effects designed for the Carl Cherry Foundation in California.

X HOUR

Objects of kinetic art, created by Munari in 1945. Fifty numbered pieces were made by Danese of Milan. The half-disks in the centre of the object are transparent and turn by clockwork, thus composing continuously changing geometrical figures.

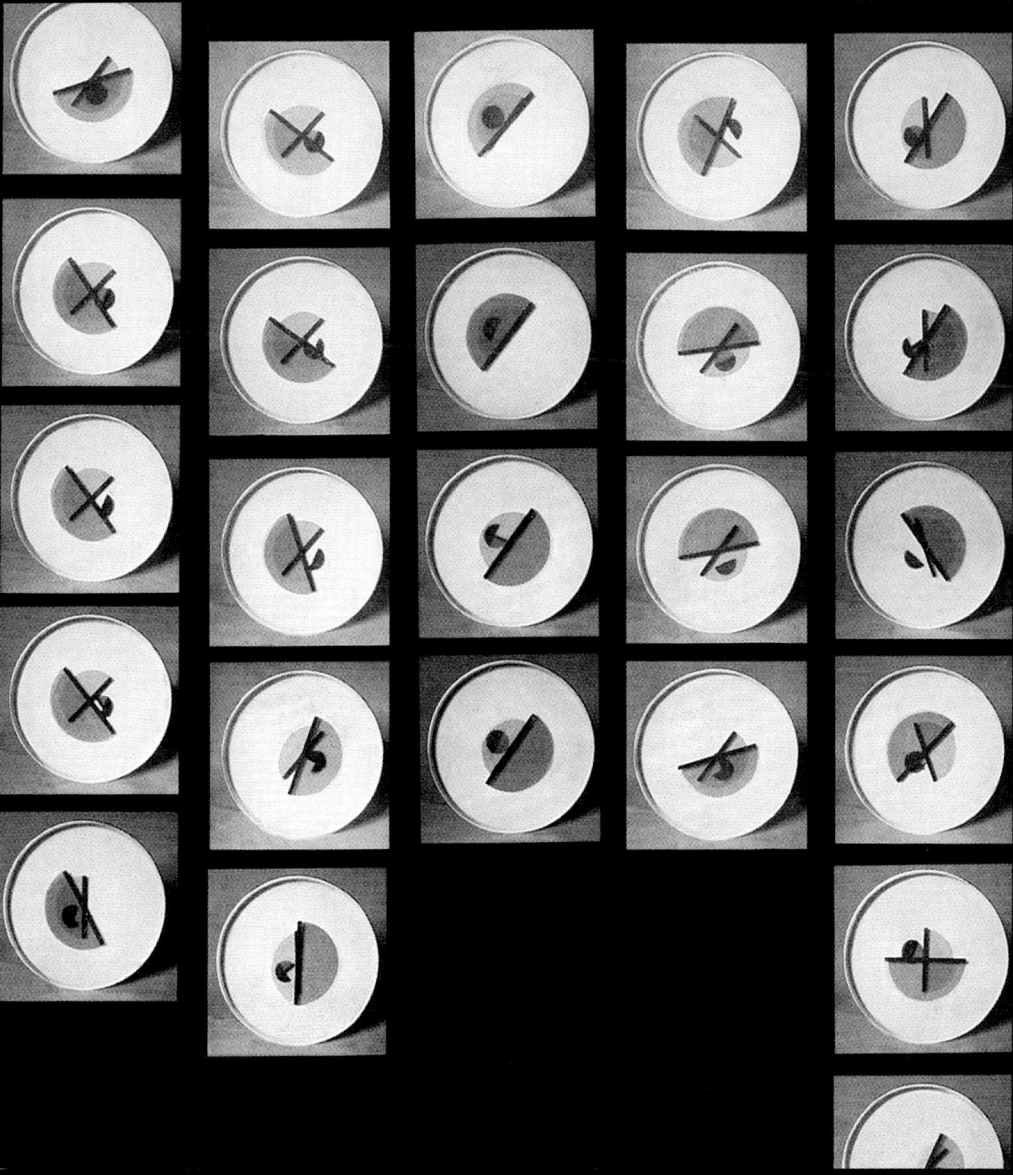

GIOVANNI PINTORI

Drawings.

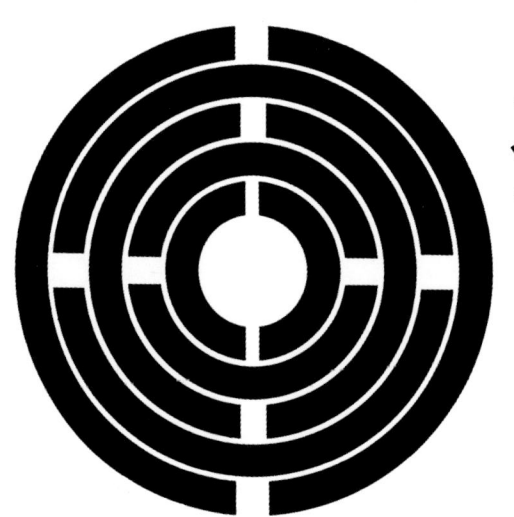

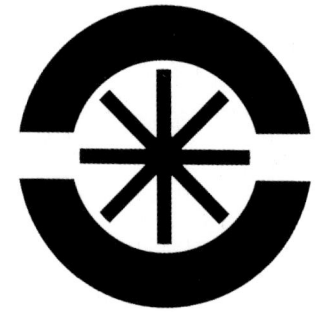

INDIAN BALL

A flexible wire structure made of circular arcs. A series of geometric figures can be obtained by changing its shape in different ways.

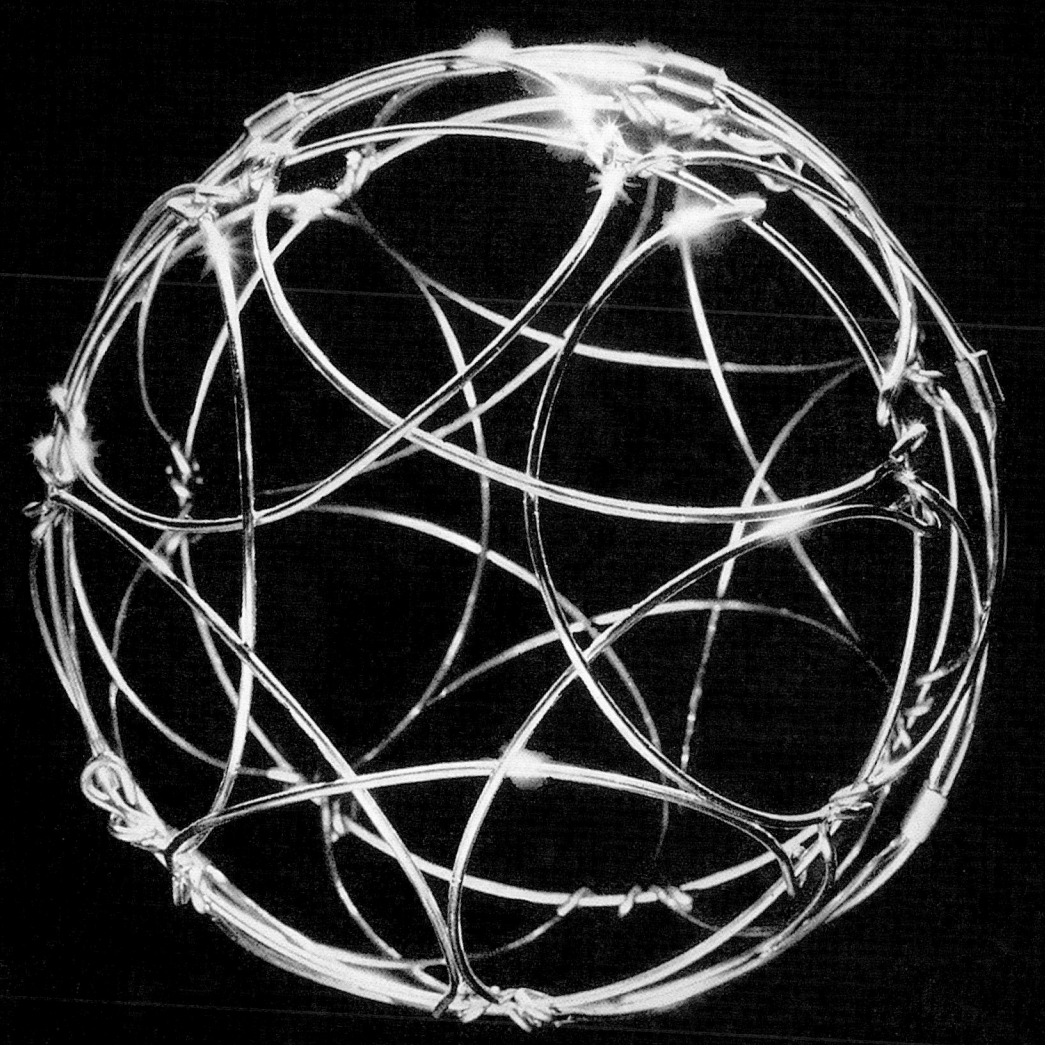

LUCA PACIOLI

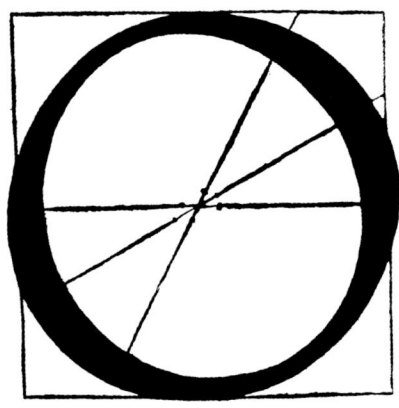

Letter of the "dignissimo antico" alphabet by Luca Pacioli.

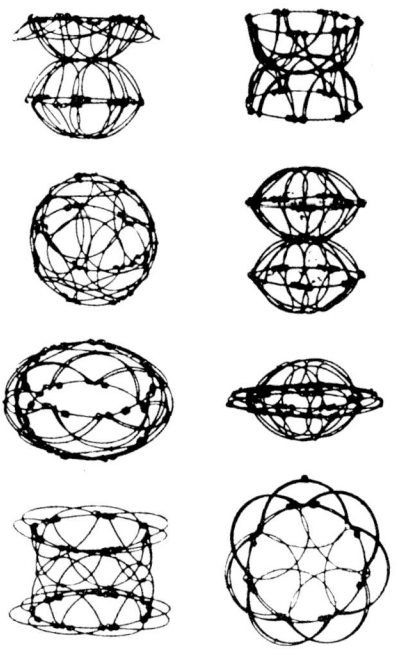

Variations on the shape of the Indian ball obtained by bending the object in various ways.

RAPHAEL

The Madonna of the Chair. Pitti Gallery, Florence.

CIRCULAR PENTAGRAM

Musical annotation of a sound-making object, with no beginning or end.

ROMANESQUE

Cross of Trinity Church at Caen.

BERNARD REDER

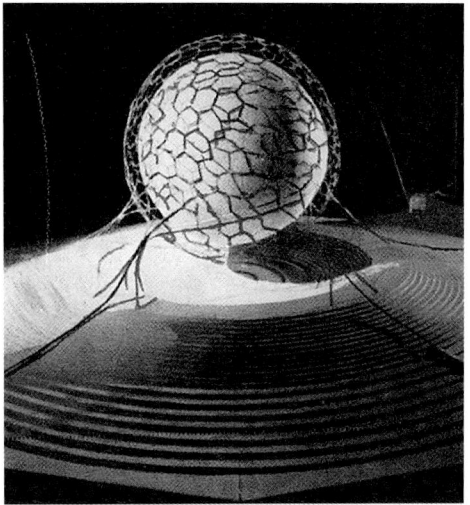

Spherical theatre. The audience is seated along a continuously moving internal spiral. The action takes place in the centre of the sphere. Very light materials need to be used in its construction.

THE WHEEL

The earliest archaeological evidence of the wheel dates back to the urban cultures of Mesopotamia. The first wheels were simply solid wooden disks firmly joined to an axle that turned along with the wheels. Later on, hubs were invented and holes were made in the solid disk. These holes gradually increased in size until the idea of spokes was introduced. Wheels with spokes existed in Asia Minor as early as 2700 BC.

THE WHEEL AS A SYMBOL

The wheel is also a symbol of the sun, of divinity and good luck and it has always been used as an ornament. To celebrate the solstice in the past blazing wheels were rolled down slopes and narrow wooden hoops were thrown into the air.

GOTHIC ROSE-WINDOW

Rose-window of the Santa Chiara Basilica at Assisi. Photo by Paolo Monti.

RADAR

Radar at the Vandenberg auxiliary station follows the path of the artificial satellites through space. The network of the radar stations extends from the US coast of the Pacific to Hawaii and north to Alaska.

CELTIC SEAL

DECREASING RADIUS

Draw a circle. Inside this, draw an equilateral triangle. Draw another circle inside the triangle. Draw a square inside the second circle. Draw another circle inside this square and follow this with a pentagon. Continue, adding an extra side to each polygon. The radius of the circles may appear to get shorter and shorter, tending to zero, but it is not so. What really happens is that the process of contraction itself tends to a limit that appears when the polygon and circle have become almost equal. The decreasing radius approaches a limit of about 1/12 of the radius of the original circle.

INCREASING RADIUS

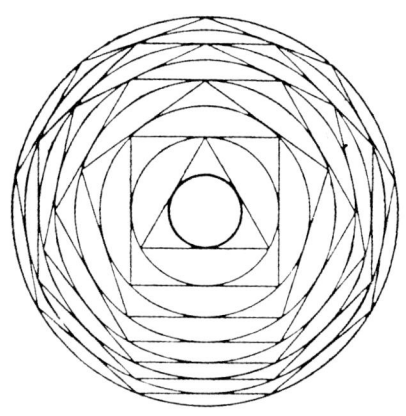

Closely connected to the problem of the decreasing radius is the problem of circumscribing rather than inscribing polygons and circles.

In this case it may appear that the radius, increasing beyond every limit, becomes infinite. Instead, it comes close to a limit of about twelve times that of the radius of the original circle.
It is interesting to note how at the limit the increasing radius has become reciprocal to the decreasing one.

POTTER'S WHEEL

The potter's wheel was known in Egypt before the beginning of the third millennium BC. Cretan craftsmen used it in the earliest stages of the Bronze Age and it was also known in many parts of India. It appeared it Europe, in France and southern Germany, in around 500 BC, while it was unknown on the American continent.

WRITING

The sign of the circle lies at the base of almost all alphabets or ideograms. These signs are common to Azilian, Megalitic, Cretan, American, Canary Island writing and cave painting.

CONNECTED SPHERES

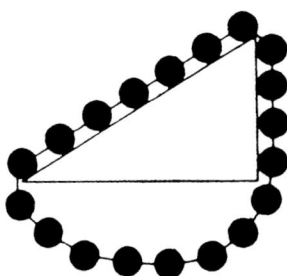

A search for perpetual motion using connected spheres. The greater weight of the spheres on the longer arm should cause the mechanism to turn.

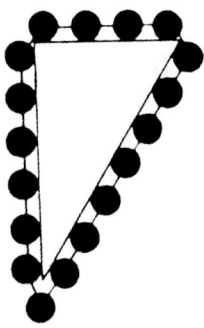

Variation of the idea with connected spheres on inclined surfaces.

COSTS

Little disks engraved on obelisks or pyramids would appear to refer to the money spent on these monuments. If the disks are arranged in a circle it means that public money was spent, if instead they are in a line it was financed by private funds.

DREAM

In his book Flying Saucers: A Modern Myth of Things Seen in the Skies, Carl Gustav Jung describes the following dream told to him by an acquaintance: ... I must stress how beautiful the sphere was with its soft grey or opaque white against the night sky. When we realised that a terrible collision was about to take place with the earth, we were, of course, afraid but it was a fear in which reverence prevailed. It was a cosmic event that caused great awe. While we were all absorbed in that vision a second and then a third sphere appeared, and then others approached at great speed. Each sphere exploded on the earth like a bomb but evidently at so great a distance that I was unable to define the nature of the explosion, or detonation, or whatever it was. In one case at least I had the impression I had seen a flash of lightning. The spheres fell all around us at intervals, but all so far away that it was impossible to perceive their destructive action. There seemed to be some sort of a danger of shrapnel effect or something similar. Then — I must have gone home — I found myself talking to a girl sitting on a wicker chair...

SHINTO

Shinto symbol: the revolving of the universe.

EMPIRE STYLE

Decorative pattern on French cloth.

GOLDEN SECTION

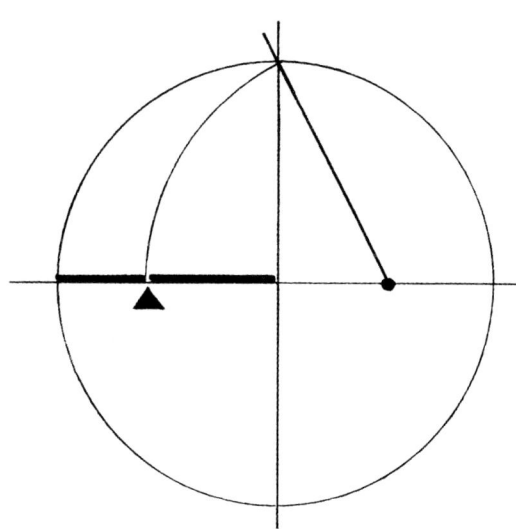

Construction of the golden section on the radium of a given circle.

STONEHENGE

Site of the famous ruins of a circular stone ring erected in around 1400 BC on Salisbury Plain in England. The 80 roughly hewn pillars and architraves that make up the main circle, each weighing about 50 tons, seem not to have been found on the site but to have come from the Prescelly Hills in Wales. The stones were physically transported overland for many miles and then were carried on rafts made of tree trunks to coastland nearer Stonehenge, where they were again moved by human force. Around the circular group of stones are other circles of holes at equal distances. Excavation work has brought to light Irish tools and weapons, gold Mycenaean jewellery and amber objects from central Europe which point to a flourishing trade with other peoples.

The central ring, still standing today, consists of a more recent circle of stones which were cut and worked nearer Stonehenge. In the centre is a large block of sandstone measuring almost 5 metres (16 ft) in length. An adventurous Greek architect might have come to Stonehenge and used the techniques learned from his people to build this stone circle, or *henge*.

A COLUMN OF SPHERES

A mobile object, Programmed Art. The spheres are held by three sheets of glass. The first sphere at the bottom sits on the pulley of a very slow motor. All the spheres turn by friction, thereby constantly changing the combination of the curved white strips painted on them. Munari 1962, Olivetti collection. Photo by Mulas.

KARLHEINZ STOCKHAUSEN

Karlheinz Stockhausen imagines an ideal auditorium for electronic music, in the form of a sphere. In the centre the public are seated on a platform built to let the sound pass through so that they can hear the music from all directions. Loudspeakers are placed all around the interior of the sphere.

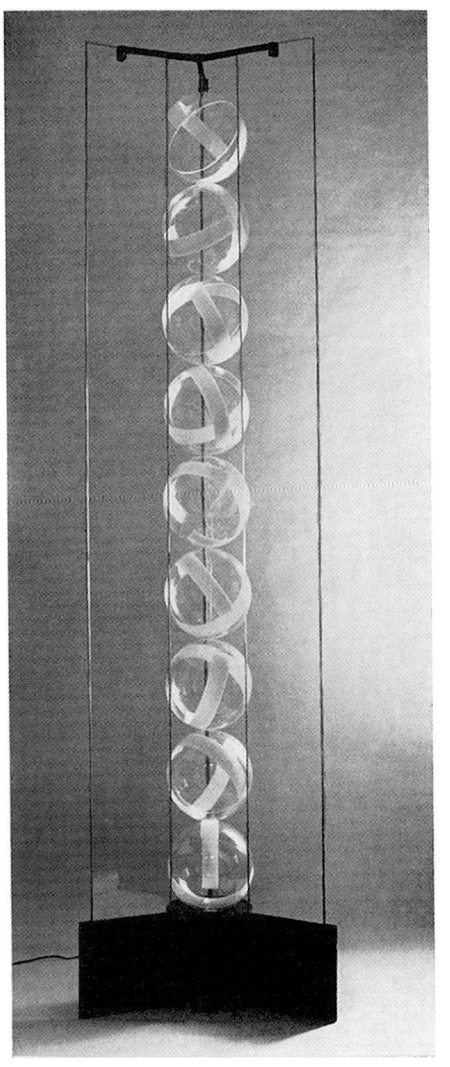

METEROLOGICAL SIGNS

From left to right: clear sky, cloudy sky, solar halo, lunar halo, rainbow, mirage, solar corona, lunar corona.

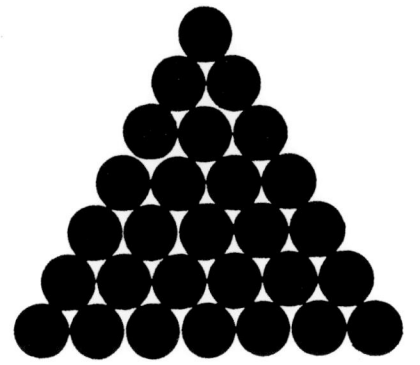

LAYER OF CIRCLES

If at all the knots of a network made up of equilateral triangles we draw some circumferences whose radii are equal to half the length of the sides of the triangles, we obtain a system of circles which touch but never overlap. This system of circles is called a layer of circles.

SAME AREA

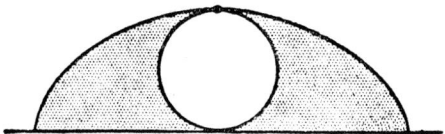

The two shaded parts have the same area as the circle that generated them.

SOLOMON

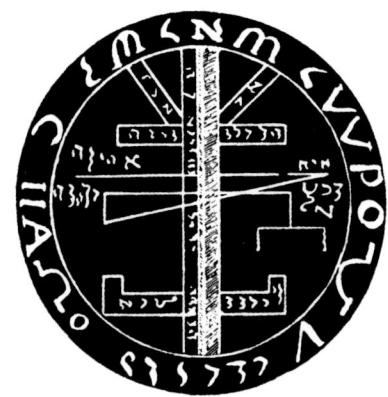

The great magic circle of Solomon.

SYMBOLS OF MARTYRDOM

CHINESE SPHERE

A carved ivory ball containing eleven other balls, one inside the other, all derived from the same block using a conical drill bit and other tools. All the balls move freely inside each other, from the smallest in the centre to the largest on the outside.

TARGET SHOOTING

TURBINES

A turbine consists of an infinite number of continuous elements arranged so that the external part is placed over a circumference and the internal parts must all incline equally with respect to the circumference. There is a whole geometry of turbines that deals with continuous groups of transformations connected to differential equations and differential geometry, introduced by Edward Kasner.

TRINITY

One of the symbols of the Trinity.

MUSLIM TALISMAN

THE ROUND TABLE

According to Breton tradition, the legendary knights of King Arthur used to sit at a round table to symbolise the fact that all were equally bound to do their duty.

TRULLI

Ancient stone dwellings, almost all of which are one storey high. They have a circular base and a conical roof. Houses with more than one room are made up of cylindrical constructions, one for each room, connected by passageways. The most famous trulli are at Alberobello and in the valley around Martina Franca.

TANGENTS

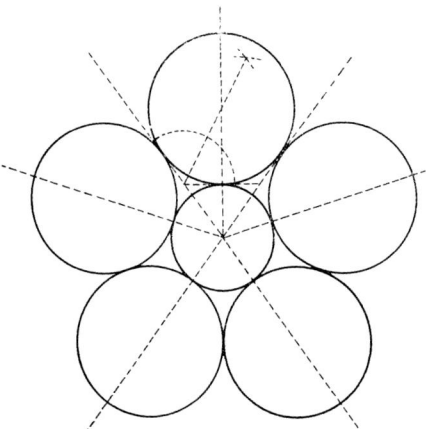

Draw several circles tangent to each other and to the outside of a given circle.

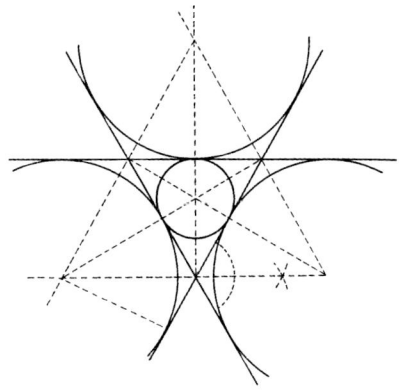

Draw four circles tangent to three straight lines which are symmetrically crossed.

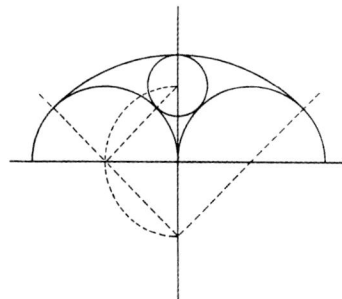

Inscribe a circle in a curvilinear isosceles triangle.

TORU TAKEMITSU

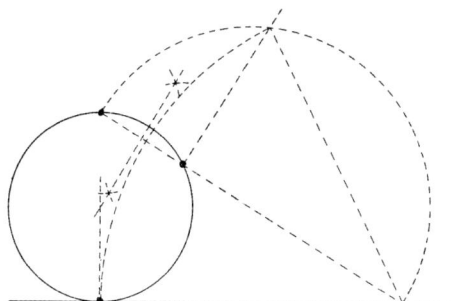

Given a straight line and two points outside it, draw a circle passing through these two points and a point on the straight line.

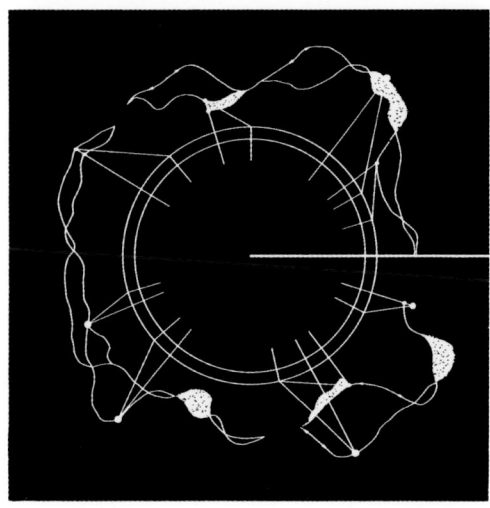

Pianist's wheel for musical annotations with no beginning and no end. A series of music sheets of the same size but with different annotations can be fitted in to create a number of variations at will, based on a scheme given by the Japanese composer.

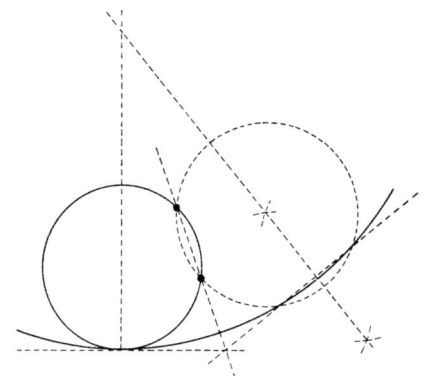

Draw a circle passing through two given points on another circle.

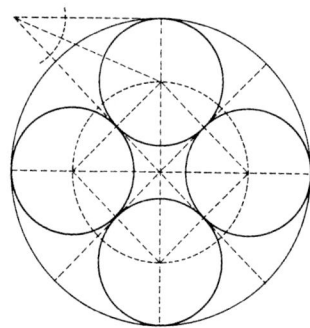

Draw several circles tangent to each other and to the inside of a given circle.

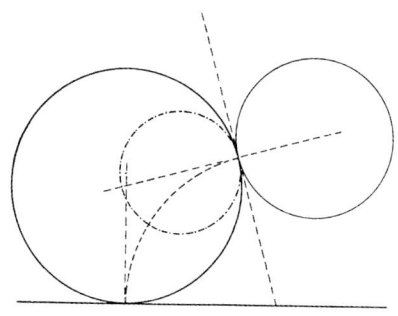

Draw two circles tangent to a straight line and to a given circle.

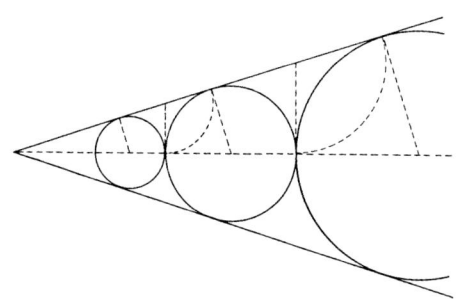

Circles tangent to each other and to the sides of a given triangle.

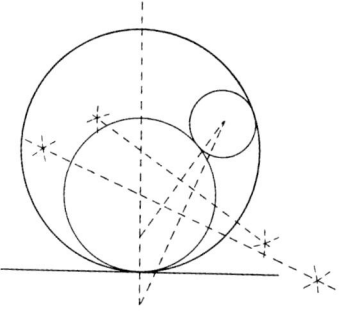

Draw a circle tangent to another one at a given point and to a straight line at another given point.

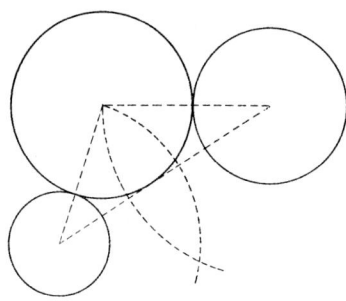

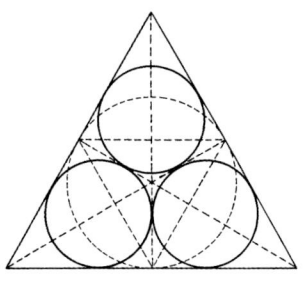

Draw a circle with a given radius, tangent to two other given circles.

Draw three circles tangent to each other and inside a given equilateral triangle.

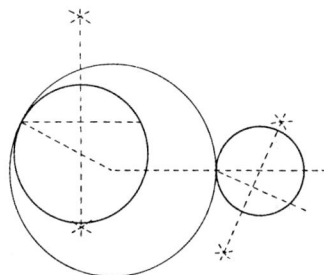

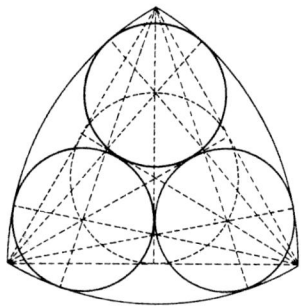

Draw a circle tangent to another one at a given point and passing through another one situated inside or outside the circle itself.

Draw three circles tangent to each other and inside a given curved equilateral triangle.

Draw two tangents common to two given circles with different radii.

ALL IS WELL

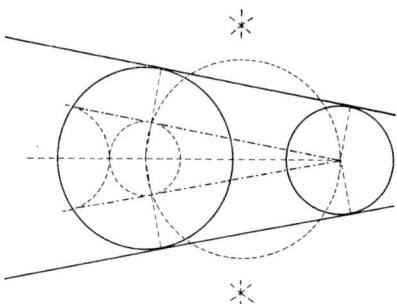

Solution A

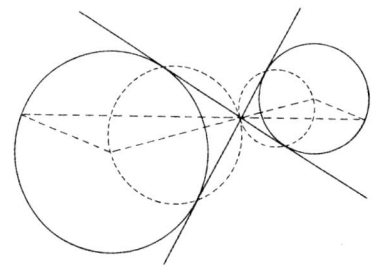

Sign of understanding among beggars.

Solution B

MARY VIEIRA

Circle + movement = forms. Object made of anodised aluminium, diameter 33 cm Basle 1953-1958.

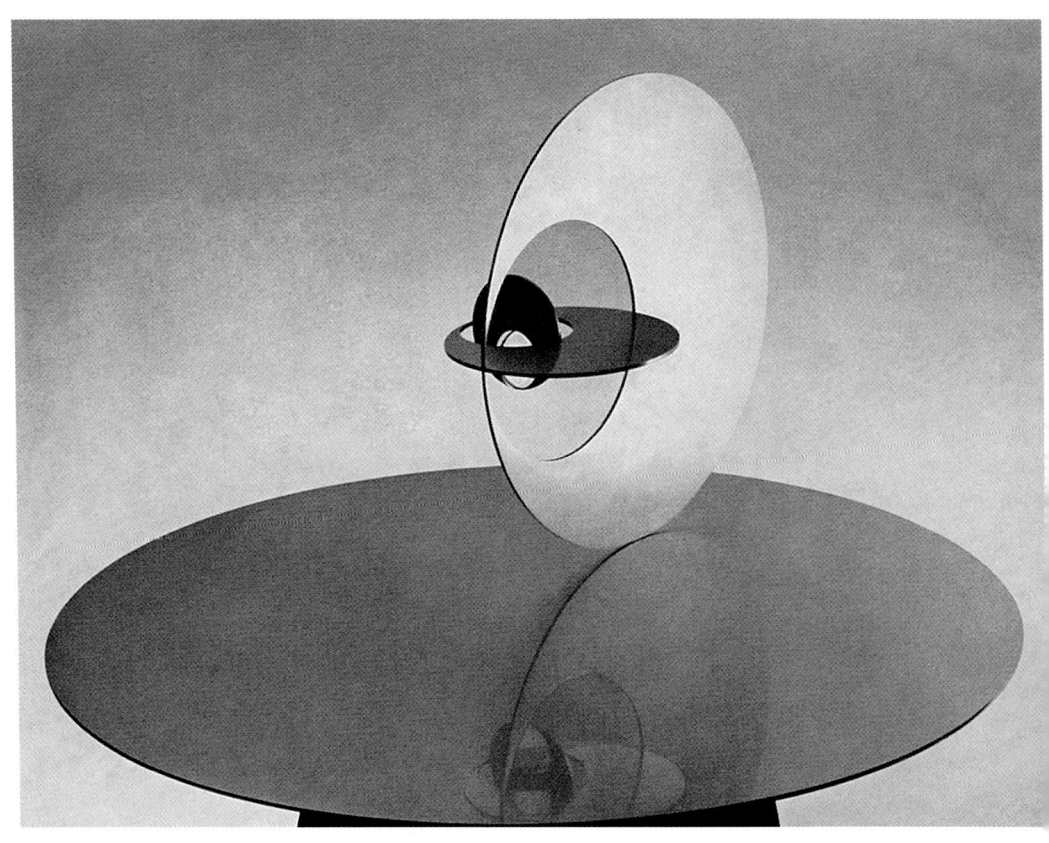

Mobile circular surfaces in their spherical space. Anodised aluminium, Mary Vieira, Basle 1953-1958.

YIN - YANG

In around 1000 BC, some anonymous Chinese sages noticed that everything in nature results from the union of two opposing forces. They called these Yin and Yang and represented them with a disk made up of two equal shapes in complementary colours, such as black and white.

Each force has its own many qualities and nuances: Yang, the positive force, represents masculinity, action, warmth, hardness, dryness, brilliancy and firmness; it is the essence of fire and light, the foot of a hill, the river source, and so on. Yin on the other hand is the negative principle: feminine, coldness, humidity, softness, darkness, mystery, secrecy, evanescence, nebulosity, turbidity and inaction. It is the essence of shadow and water, the north side of a hill, the mouth of a river.... Depending on whether Yang or Yin prevails, things appear differently: Yang is predominant in the sky, Yin on the earth. One of the principles may prevail in a given thing at a certain time and then the other may dominate.

LUDOLPH VAN CEULEN

A famous German mathematician. In 1596 he calculated the value of π to 35 decimal places. The result he obtained was 3.14159 26535 89793 23846. According to his wishes the number was engraved on his headstone as his epitaph.

MARQUIS OF WORCESTER

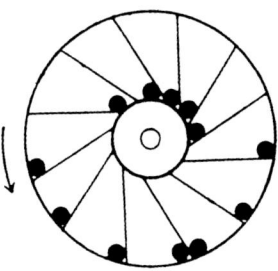

Model of a perpetual motion machine. In 1663 the Marquis published a collection of his very bizarre inventions. He became famous however for his sauce.

FAN

A series of equal sticks determines the shape of this type of folding fan.

MONOCYCLE

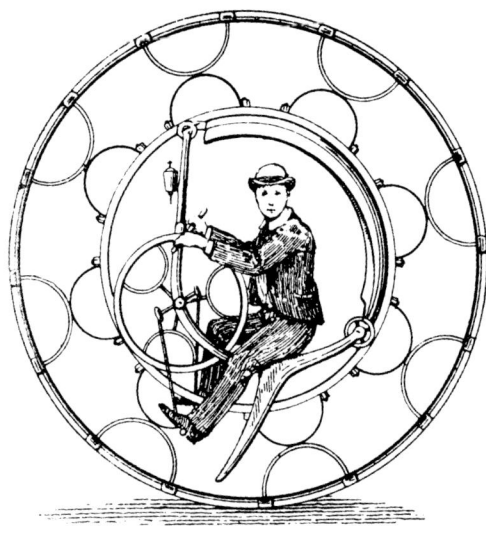

American model.

INDEX

As all the subjects in this book have been arranged in alphabetical order (as far as make-up allows) no index is necessary.

Books and publications consulted:

N. I. Lobacevskij: I NUOVI PRINCIPI DELLA GEOMETRIA. Einaudi, Torino 1955.
S. I. Vavilov: L'OCCHIO E IL SOLE. Feltrinelli, Milano 1955.
Hugo Steinhaus: MATHEMATICAL SNAPSHOTS. Oxford University Press, New York 1960.
ENCICLOPEDIA DELLA CIVILTÀ ATOMICA. Il Saggiatore, Milano 1959.
David Diringer: L'ALFABETO NELLA STORIA DELLA CIVILTÀ. Barbera, Firenze 1953.
Rudolf Koch: THE BOOK OF SIGNS. Dover publications inc., New York 1955.
Ernst Lehner: THE PICTURE BOOK OF SYMBOLS. Penn, New York 1956.
ARTE PROGRAMMATA. Olivetti, Milano.
Celeste Malavasi: SETTECENTOCINQUANTA MECCANISMI. Hoepli, Milano 1937.
Camillo Bruno: IL PROBLEMA DEL MOTO PERPETUO. Lavagnolo, Torino.
Paul Klee: TEORIA DELLA FORMA E DELLA FIGURAZIONE. Feltrinelli, Milano 1956.
Helmut Th. Bossert: ENCYCLOPEDIE DE L'ORNEMENT. Albert Morancé, Paris 1955.
Carl G. Jung: SU COSE CHE SI VEDONO NEL CIELO. Bompiani, Milano 1960.
Edward Kasner / James Newman: MATEMATICA E IMMAGINAZIONE. Bompiani, Milano 1948.
Alexander Speltz: LES STYLES DE L'ORNEMENT. Hoepli, Milano 1949.
Julius E. Lips: L'ORIGINE DELLE COSE. Sansoni, Firenze 1947.
Pierre Schaeffer: A LA RECHERCHE D'UNE MUSIQUE CONCRETE. Editions du Seuil, Paris 1952.
Gyorgy Kepes: THE NEW LANDSCAPE. Paul Theobald, Chicago 1956.
Michel Huet et K. Fodeba: LES HOMMES DE LA DANSE. Editions Clairefontaine, Lausanne 1954.
Umberto Eco e G. B. Zorzoli: STORIA ILLUSTRATA DELLE INVENZIONI. Bompiani, Milano 1960.
IL MONDO DELLA NATURA. Mondadori, Milano 1962.
Robert W. Marks: THE DYMAXION WORLD OF BUCKMINSTER FULLER. Reinhold, New York 1960.
Edouard Fer: SOLFEGE DE LA COULEUR. Dunod, Paris.
ARCHITECTURES FANTASTIQUES. L'architecture d'aujourd'hui, Paris.
SCIENTIFIC AMERICAN. Scientific American inc., New York.
Matila C. Ghyka: ESTETIQUE DES PROPORTIONS. Gallimard, Paris 1946.
Sigfried Giedion: BREVIARIO DI ARCHITETTURA. Garzanti, Milano 1961.
David Hilbert e S. Cohn-Vossen: GEOMETRIA INTUITIVA. Boringhieri, Torino 1952.
Wassily Kandinsky: DELLA SPIRITUALITÀ NELL'ARTE. Religio, Roma 1946.

THE CIRCLE
DISCOVERY OF THE CIRCLE
Bruno Munari

©1964 Bruno Munari
All rights reserved by Maurizio Corraini s.r.l.

No part of this book may be reproduced or transmitted in any
form or by any means (electronic or mechanical, including
photocopying, recording or any information retrieval system)
without permission in writing from the publisher.

Original first edition published in 1964 Scheiwiller, Milano
Maurizio Corraini first edition 2006
The publisher will be at complete disposal to whom might be related
to the unidentified sources printed in this book.

Translation corrainiStudio
Printed in Italy by Intergrafica Verona
May 2006

Maurizio Corraini s.r.l.
Via Ippolito Nievo, 7/A
46100 Mantova
Tel. 0039 0376 322753
Fax 0039 0376 365566
e-mail: sito@corraini.com
www.corraini.com